THE
BEE FRIENDLY
GARDEN

THE BEE FRIENDLY GARDEN

Ted Hooper & Mike Taylor

alphabet
&image
PUBLISHERS

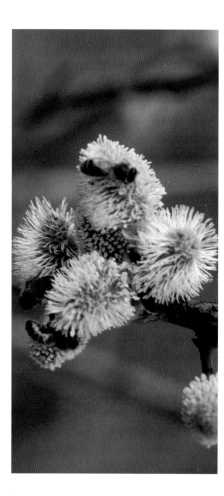

Alphabet and Image Publishers
77 High Street
Totnes
Devon TQ9 5PB

Published by Alphabet and Image Publishers 2006

ISBN 1-899296-29-8
ISBN 978-1-899296-29-3

Text © Ted Hooper and Mike Taylor 2006
Design and layout © A&I Ltd
The moral rights of the authors have been asserted.

Photography with thanks to Tony Birks-Hay and Mike Taylor.
Front cover picture David R. Frazier Photolibrary, Inc.
With thanks to contributor to John Horsey for Dealing with Pests section.

A CIP catalogue record for this book is available from the British Library.

The publishers and authors disclaim any injury, damage, loss or liability connected
with the use of the activities in this book. There may be unintentional errors or
omissions. In this case, please contact the publishers.

Some of the text and pictures first appeared in *The Beekeeper's Garden*, first
published in 1988 by Alphabooks.

Printed and bound in China by Compass Press.

Contents

Key to abbreviations used in plant A-Z

✓	particularly bee friendly plants
B./C.	bulb/corm
nec./Pol.	nectar and/or pollen source
shr.	shrub
H.	herbaceous
B./C.	bulb/corm
A(h).	hardy annual
salt tol.	coastal/salt-spray tolerant
Bien.	biennial
Ann.	annual
A(h)	hardy annual
ht.	height metric/imperial
dist.	suggested spacing between plants of same species
month-month	flowering months, e.g. Jul.-Sep.
acid	requires acid soil
alk	requires alkaline soil
wet	requires damp situation
dry	requires dry situation
full sun/semi-shade/shade	optimum situation

Introduction

In recent years gardeners have become more interested in preserving wildlife than destroying it. Many are learning to differentiate between insects which are beneficial, or neutral, and those which do sufficient damage to be destroyed as pests. In particular there is a growing interest in bees, of all sorts, which are continuously working plants for nectar and pollen. Bees do essential work in the production of seed and fruit, and their pollinating activities contribute to the survival of wild flowers. Gardeners who are able to become beekeepers also become more closely associated with these interesting insects, and benefit from their labours of pollination as well as honey and wax production.

Conversely, many beekeepers who start as unconvinced gardeners become enthusiastic when trying to understand the difference in value of particular flowers to the honey bee, usually starting with field crops and the wild flowers of their area. These are the flowers which produce the beekeeper's honey crop, and most beekeepers become reasonably well-informed amateur botanists. Interest then spreads to the wild flowers to plant in their own garden, and close observation to decide which plants are most attractive to their bees. This is most important in suburban and urban areas, where the cultivated trees and flowers in private gardens and parks provide the largest proportion of forage plants from which bees will obtain nectar.

Beekeepers will not only want to grow bee forage flowers themselves, but should try to persuade all their neighbours, the local council, parks department and highway authority to plant a reasonable proportion of bee forage plants, as this will be a very significant factor in the size of their honey harvest. In fact, urban and suburban areas are very good for honey production, their crop varying less in size from year to year than do honey crops in rural districts.

Here is the basic information required by beekeepers who wish to increase the value of their garden to honey bees, and by gardeners who wish to attract bees to the garden. Anyone thinking of starting beekeeping should join their local beekeeping association. Their meetings in the winter provide talks by well-known beekeepers and, in summer, garden meetings where they will see colonies handled and discussed. They will meet local beekeepers who will be helpful and suggest sources of bees. The societies usually supply seeds and sometimes plants at a reduced price, and organise the exchange of plants between members.

Bee Friendly Plants A–Z

A bee stealing nectar through the hole cut by bumble-bees in a broad bean flower. Similar holes are visible on the other flowers. The black spot in the top right of the picture on the triangular stipule marks the extra-floral nectary

There are so many plants suitable for a bee friendly garden that a large estate would be needed to accommodate them all. Several encyclopedias would also be necessary to describe the variety of plants in sufficient detail for gardeners and beekeepers to be able to choose between them.

The average garden is unlikely to be large enough to accommodate sizeable trees or shrubs so carefully select medium to small plants which will provide pollen and/or nectar from February to November. Bearing in mind that there are nearly always dwarf forms of most genera, even a pocket handkerchief-sized garden can provide this length season of interest for the bees. For would-be or serious beekeepers, few small or even medium-sized gardens can provide sufficient nectar or pollen to significantly contribute to a colony's development, except in the case of early-spring or late-autumn sources of pollen. Try to persuade neighbours and parks departments, or anyone growing flowers within a couple of miles, to grow a number of those mentioned in the text. This will make a considerable difference to the well-being of the colonies and the quantity of honey available at the end of the year. Even giving away a few plants from your own garden can be well worthwhile.

Remember that full sun will encourage bees to work the flowers; plants in shade rarely attract them in any numbers. Bees do not like cold winds either, so some shelter is also desirable. Plants with double flowers have been excluded from the plant lists, because the frustration experienced by bees when attempting to get at the pollen or nectar is obvious.

KITCHEN GARDEN

The honey bee will mainly be found in flower and fruit gardens. Of plants grown in the kitchen garden, only those which are grown for seed, or for the fruit (e.g. marrow) are of interest to bees and these amount to only two or three plants. The broad bean plant, *Vicia faba*, and the scarlet runner bean, *Phaseolus coccineus*, supply both nectar and pollen for the bees, and need to attract them as they require bee pollination, particularly the runner bean, to set seed. Where these vegetables are grown commercially, colonies of honey bees are often hired to provide good pollination. *V. faba* is unique in that honey bees work it in three different ways. Pollen collectors and some nectar gatherers go in from the front of the flower and these effect pollination. Short-tongued bumble-bees, *Bombus* species, cut a hole in the base of the flower to get at the nectar and, after this has been done, honey bees work through the holes as well. Finally, the honey bees work the black spot on the stipules, which is an extra-floral nectary and at times produces a nectar which is higher in sugar content than that in the flower itself.

It is often possible to see all three methods of work occurring at one time. The resulting honey is rich in flavour and medium in colour. The tips of the later spring sowings are commonly plastered with blackfly, *Aphis fabae*, during July and August. To avoid having to spray, nip out the tips of the plants either at the first sign of attack or once four tiers of pods have formed.

Phaseolus coccineus has an extremely complex flower and therefore needs a sophisticated pollinating insect, such as a bee, to effect entry and bring about the pollination without which only a very tiny amount of seed is set and pods retained. *P. vulgaris*, the French bean, has white flowers which are self-pollinating and are of no interest to the bee. Similarly the garden pea, *Pisum sativum*, provides neither nectar nor pollen and is completely self-pollinating.

The only other plants normally found in the kitchen garden which are of interest to bees are the gourds such as vegetable marrow, ridge cucumbers and gherkins. These provide nectar and pollen in quantity, but the number of flowers per plant is so small that they are not always searched out by the bees. Should the gardener allow *brassicas* to remain in the soil and flower, the bees will be really pleased, as they are very attractive and provide good quantities of both pollen and nectar.

Abelia Nec./Pol. Shr.
ht: 1.25m *4ft* dist: 1m *3ft* full sun.
Abelia is a real charmer; its clusters of bell-shaped five-petalled flowers making it a very valuable garden and bee plant. The brown or pink sepals are showy in their own right and are very persistent, remaining long after the flowers have fallen. They are especially attractive when viewed against the dark evergreen or semi-evergreen leaves.

Abelias are very easy to grow, even on heavy soils, as long as the drainage is good. Their one weakness is that they are not entirely hardy, and most species require the shelter of a wall or other plants; this is not easily achieved, since they must also have full sun. Common winter damage amounts to branches being killed back, but these will usually sprout again from near their bases. The first new shoots may not appear until June, in common with many other severely frost-damaged plants. Cuttings taken in August root very easily, and these can be an 'insurance policy' against a really hard winter.

A. chinensis Jul.–Aug. Deciduous. The fragrant flowers are white with a rose flush, pink sepals.

'Edward Goucher' Jul.–Sep. Evergreen. This semi-evergreen cultivar has purplish-pink flowers. Deciduous

A. schumanii May–Aug. Deciduous. Flowers rose-pink, up to 2.5cm (1in) long.

Acer (Maples) Nec./Pol. Deciduous.
Full sun, semi-shade.
There is a large number of species and an increasing number of cultivars in this variable and decorative genus of deciduous trees and shrubs. Some attain heights of over 30m (100ft), while others may reach only 2–2.25m (6–8ft). Fortunately some of the larger types are frequently found in the wild, where their free-flowering characteristics ensure a good 'crop' of early nectar and pollen. The nectar is secreted by a fleshly green disc, to which the stamens are attached. If the eight greenish-yellow, spreading petals are removed, the whole structure looks rather like an eight-legged stool. The double-winged seeds, or 'helicopters' are familiar to all and are freely produced by most species.

Most Acers are grown for their bark, leaf shape or autumn colour, but the flowers are very showy in some species. The leaves are typically palmate, as in the maple leaf emblem of Canada, but they may have three or as many as five lobes, depending on species.

A. campestre (Hedge or Field Maple) T. ht: 6–12m *20–40ft* Apr. Occasionally up to 21m (70ft), this tree is more usually 4.5–6m (15–20ft), and frequently seen, as the common name implies, in hedges. It has the typical palmate leaf, up to 10cm (4in) across, and small green flowers held erect at first, and then pendulous. In autumn the leaves turn a clear golden yellow. A beautiful tree if you have the space; if not, it's perfect for a hedgerow.

A. capillipes T. ht: 9m *30ft* May. A rather small tree whose green bark has attractive white striations. The flowers are yellow and the new growth is an attractive coral red. The species *pensylvanicum* is similar and is more suitable for slightly acid soils.

A. griseum (Paperback Maple) T. ht: 7.5m *25ft* May. One of the most beautiful of all garden trees, with bark that flakes away to reveal the varied coppery brown colouration beneath. The three-lobed leaves often turn a beautiful red or scarlet in autumn. Pendulous flowers.

A. negundo (Box Elder) T. ht: 13.3m *45ft* May. A rather fast-growing tree, with bright-green young shoots and leaves with three–five leaflets. Most frequently seen in its less vigorous form 'Elgans', which has showy yellow marginal leaf variegation. The male and female flowers bloom on separate plants, so try if possible to obtain a male, since the females bear no pollen.

A. palmatum (Japanese Maple) Shr. ht: 9m *30ft* dist: 3m *10ft* May–Jun., acid. Japanese maples will grow to 6–9m (20–30ft) if well protected by other trees, but they are more usually seen as smaller, relatively slow-growing shrubs, some 1.25–4.5m (4–15ft) in height. They are beautiful and elegant plants even in winter, when the dense twiggy growth can be seen to best effect. The leaves, which turn to brilliant reds and oranges in autumn, have five–seven toothed lobes. The cultivar 'Heptalobum Osakazuki' has an incredible mixture of fiery red and orange autumn leaf colouration. Shelter from wind, particularly in spring, is essential if the new growth of all the *palmatum* cultivars is not to be badly scorched.

'Atropurpureum' Shr. ht: 2–4.5m *6–15ft* dist: 2–2.5m *6–8ft*. Certainly the most frequently grown cultivar and deservedly so, with its bronze-crimson leaf colouration.

'Dissectum' Shr. ht: 1.25m *4ft* dist: 1.25m *4ft*. Much less vigorous than most of the other cultivars in this genus, this has attractive much-divided toothed leaves.

There are several other cultivars with purple, yellow and even variegated foliage. All are first-class garden plants in a sheltered spot with acid soil.

A. platanoides T. ht: 21m *70ft* Apr. The Norway maple, with its erect clusters of bright yellow-green flowers, is a familiar sight in Europe's April hedgerows and, although the individual flowers are small they are present in sufficient numbers to create quite an impact, especially when seen cheek by jowl with blackthorn. Unless you have an estate or very large garden, then this species, with its wonderful buttercup-yellow autumn colouration, is best admired in a natural woodland setting. Choose instead one of a number of excellent cultivars, slower growing but ultimately still very large trees, which have found their way into many gardens.

'Erectum' ht: 6–9m *20–30ft*. Its erect habit and slower growth make this a most suitable cultivar for the garden.

'Crimson King' ht: 12m *40ft*. Dark-purple leaves and similarly coloured seeds.

'Schwedleri' ht: 12m *40ft*. The leaves and young growth are a rich crimson-purple, paler beneath and very handsome towards the end of the flowering period.

A. pseudoplatanus (Sycamore) T. ht: 24m *80ft* May. A very common tree throughout the British Isles and woodland mountainous areas of Europe (and present even in very exposed areas), often in sufficient numbers for it to be a considerable source of nectar on warm early summer days. Again, like the Norway maple, do not contemplate planting this giant in your own garden, but choose instead one of the excellent slow-growing cultivars.

'Brilliantissimum' ht: 4.5m *15ft*. Rather slow growing and mop-headed, this is without doubt one of the very best small trees. The new spring growth is a gorgeous soft pink streaked with lime green, against which the large clusters of pendulous yellow-green flowers can be viewed. Unfortunately, the leaves turn a rather more mundane green as the summer progresses.

'Prinz Handjery' ht: 6m *20ft*. Rather similar to 'Brilliantissimum', but with leaves purple-tinged beneath.

Achillea (Yarrow) Nec. H.
Full sun.
Given good drainage and a sunny position there are few plants that will reward you and your bees with more flowers for such little effort. The individual 'flowers' (broad ray-florets variable in number) are about 6mm (0.33in) diameter, but there is usually a very large number of them forming each flat-topped head, and a good number of the stiffly erect flower stems to each plant.

Most of the species are clump-forming and the long, deeply bisected basal leaves (rather like hairy fern fronds) usually come through the winter unscathed. The leaves are pungent making them very pleasant. The flowering stems and flower heads dry well (except possibly for *millefolium* cultivars).

A. ageratifolia ht: 15cm *6in* dist: 23cm *9in* Jun.–Jul. Silvery leaves, white flower heads.

A. filipendulina 'Gold Plate' ht: 1.2m *4ft* dist: 60–73cm *2–2.5ft* Jun.–Aug. Large golden-yellow flower heads.

'Coronation Gold' ht: 91cm *3ft* dist: 60cm *2ft* Jun.–Aug. Similar to 'Gold Plate'.

'Moonshine' ht: 60cm *2ft* dist: 45cm *18in* Jun.–Aug. A beautiful cultivar with feathery silver foliage and bright yellow flowers.

A. millefolium 'Cerise Queen' ht: 75cm *2.5ft* dist: 45cm *18in* May–Sep. Loose heads of cerise-red flowers.

'Lilac Beauty' ht: 30cm *2ft* dist: 45cm *18in* May–Sep. Lilac flowers.

A. serrata 'W.B. Child' ht: 30cm *2ft* dist: 45cm *18in* Jun. and Sep. Large, white, loose flower heads.

A. tomentosa ht: 15cm *6in* dist: 23cm *9in* Jun.–Aug. Very 'woolly' foliage and deep yellow flower heads.

Achilleas spread quickly and friends are usually only too willing to give pieces away in an attempt to control their expansionist habits.

Aesculus Nec./Pol. Deciduous.
Full sun.
There are few trees that can rival the magnificence of an eighty-foot horse-chestnut in full flower. But there are some Aesculus of less massive proportions with equally beautiful flowers. All produce nectar freely and are enthusiastically worked by bees, as is obvious from the brick-red pollen loads being taken into the hive. Select the species planted with care, as the red horse-chestnut *A. carnea* does at times poison bees working it. Bumble-bees are more readily affected, but often the ground under the tree will be littered with bees unable to fly. The bees are often attacked by birds, and will be seen to have lost the ends of their abdomens.

The large flowers, or candles as they are commonly known, are broadly pyramidal in shape and are made up of many individual florets, the corollas of which have four or five unequal flared petals and protruding, upwardly-curved stamens. The large, five-to-seven-lobed leaves are coarsely toothed, distinct and handsome.

The large sticky buds of the horse-chestnut are conspicuous and attractive, as are the green spiny cases that hold the conkers, which usually fall after a few sharp frosts.

All Aesculus colour well in the autumn, usually in the gold and russet colour range.

A. hippocastanum (Horse-chestnut) T. ht: 24m *80ft* May. Far too large for most gardens, so hope your neighbours will have it, for you and the bees to enjoy. The white, mostly male flowers are about 30cm (12in) long, with yellow spots, which turn pink as they age.

A. parviflora Shr. ht: 2.5m *8ft* dist: 2.5–2.75m *8–9ft* Jul.–Aug. White flowers with red anthers and, like *pavia* below, really grown as a shrub.

A. pavia (Red Buckeye) ht: 3m *10ft* dist: 3m *10ft* Jun.–Jul. Crimson flowers up to 15cm (6in) long.

Althaea rosea

Alcea syn. **Althaea** (Hollyhock) Nec./Pol. H.
ht: 2–2.5m *6–8ft* dist: 60–90cm *2–3ft* Jul.–Sep., full sun.
This is a real cottage garden plant, with tall elegant flower spikes, now all too infrequently seen, particularly in its most interesting and attractive single form. The large five-petalled, saucer-like flowers are very showy and have a satin-like sheen. The basal flowers open first, and the large club-like mass of stamens are typical of the Malvaceae family and bear masses of very large pollen grains. The bees work it mainly for the pollen, especially useful late in the season, and bees can be seen returning to the hive covered with it, sometimes with a distinct white mark on their backs in a place they do not seem able to reach to clean. The leaves are generally grey-green and quite rough-textured.

A. ficifolia A variable species with white, yellow or orange flowers up to 10cm (4in) in diameter, and deeply lobed leaves. Biennial or short-lived perennial.

A. rosea Available in a mixture of colours – pink, crimson, rose, cream and white; the leaves are broadly heart-shaped.

'Nigra' ht: 2m *6ft*. A dull red-black.

Be warned that most, if not all, hollyhocks sold by garden centres will be doubles, so you may need to raise your own from seed sown outdoors in spring; the resultant plants will normally flower in the following spring. Plant them into their final positions as soon as possible, since they are reputed not to like root disturbance.

Alchemilla (Lady's Mantle) Nec./Pol. H.
Jun.–Sep., full fun, semi-shade.
The delicacy of the leaves, and especially the flowers, belies the tough adaptability of this superb tufted plant which thrives in both sun and shade or wet and dry soils alike. The individual flowers are small, yellow or yellow-green and borne in great numbers in clusters (similar to *Gypsophila* but not quite as loose), held well above the rounded and serrated leaves. A most attractive and easily grown plant. It can have very small leaves borne on the most beautiful thin wiry red stems. As with all Alchemillas, the papery brown stipules are a distinctive feature. You are very unlikely to find more than two species on sale in most garden centres of the delicate-looking Alchemilla, much loved by flower-arrangers. All species tend to seed freely and become invasive, so remove the old flower heads to avoid being taken over.

A. alpina (Alpine Lady's Mantle) ht: 20cm *8in* dist: 45cm *18in*. Do not be fooled by its name into thinking this is not a vigorous and even rampant grower – it is. The flowers are more green than yellow, and bloom in dense clusters; leaves are silvery beneath and their margins are silkily hairy.

A. mollis ht: 45cm *18in* dist: 45–60cm *18–24in*. A rather taller-growing species with larger, pale-green, softly hairy leaves.

Allium Nec./Pol. B./C.
Full sun, shade.
The ornamental forms of the culinary types – leeks, garlic, chives and the common onion – have a wide colour range and vary from the small rounded flower heads of *A. flavum* to the more massive heads of *A. christophii*. The individual flowers which make up the flower heads are star-like, with six narrow, shallowly spoon-shaped petals around the six stamens and a single stigma above the ovary. This is circular at first, but swells into a three–five lobed 'cluster' once the seed starts to form, making these forms very attractive as dried flowers. The leaves are normally long and narrow, but may be tubular, triangular or flat in section. In the common wild ramson (*A. ursinum*) the leaves are oval with very long stalks; the leaves of *A. christophii* are lance-shaped and stalkless.

A variable genus, but well worth growing. Try not to trample on the plants or crush them in any way or you will carry the smell around with you for some time! (Fortunately neither the honey nor the dried flower heads carry the typical onion aroma.) Most species are worked for nectar, and onion honey is produced in California and elsewhere where the crops are grown for seed.

A. flatuense ht: 1m *3ft* dist: 23cm *9in* Jun.–Jul. Tennis-ball size flower heads of pale lilac, leaves blue-green and broadly strap-shaped.

A. cernuum ht: 30cm *1ft* dist: 15cm *6in* Jun.–Jul. Nodding heads of deep-pink flowers.

A. christophii syn. *albopilosum* ht: 60cm *2ft* dist: 23cm *9in* Jun.–Jul. Massive flower heads of pale purple with a metallic sheen.

A. flavum ht: 23cm *9in* dist: 15cm *6in* Jul.–Aug. Yellow bell-shaped flowers carried on small heads above blue-grey foliage.

A. moly ht: 30cm *1ft* dist: 15cm *6in* Jun.–Jul. Bright-yellow flower heads 7cm (3in) or so across, and grey-green leaves. A handsome but vigorous plant that should be given the company of other 'invaders' to help keep it in check – try Nepeta or some of the mat-forming Thymes.

A. narcissiflorum ht: 20cm *8in* dist: 10cm *4in* Jun.–Jul. A charming dwarf species with nodding pink flowers.

A. oreophilum ostrowskianum ht: 20cm *8in* dist: 15cm *6in* Jun.–Jul. Deep rose-pink flower heads up to 10cm (4in) across.

A. schoenoprasum (Chives) ht: 23–45cm *9–18in* dist: 30–60cm *1–2ft* Jun.–Aug. A very underrated and highly decorative plant with cylindrical leaves and tight clusters of mauve flowers. Grown as an ornamental plant in its own right, it is avidly worked by bees for nectar and pollen. There is enormous variation between the various strains of this species: 46cm (18in) is not an uncommon height.

A. tuberosum ht: 45cm *18in* dist: 30cm *1ft* Sep.–Oct. A white-flowered species.

Alstroemeria (Peruvian Lily) H. Nec./Pol.
ht: 1–1.25m *3–4ft* dist: 70–75cm *28–30in* Jun.–Aug, full sun.
The masses of six-pointed trumpet-like flowers, 6–9cm (2–3in) in diameter, are borne in clusters at the top of erect leafy stems, and with their satin-like sheen are quite beautiful. The inner petals are often gorgeously veined, splotched and suffused with a contrasting colour. They are popular and easily available.

The tuberous root system is easily damaged, so always buy container-grown specimens. As with many plants with fleshy roots, drainage must be good if rotting-off losses are to be avoided.

Allium. The smell of the plant does not taint honey. However, if you crush a few flowers, the smell will linger

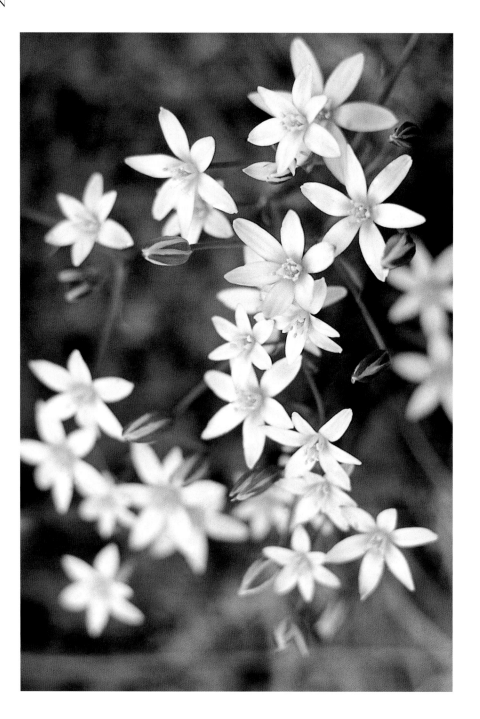

A. aurantiaca 'Dover Orange' Orange-red flowers.

'Ligu hybrids' A really superb mixture of shades of pink to golden-orange to orange-red. These slightly more vigorous hybrids are now far more commonly available than any of the older species or cultivars.

Alyssusm saxatile (Golden Alyssum) Nec./Pol. Evergreen.
ht: 23cm *9in* dist: 30–456cm *12–18in* Apr.–Jun., dry, full sun.
The bright-yellow flowers are a rather harsh colour, but April can be a pretty dull time for the garden and bees alike, and the masses of these small cruciferous flowers, completely obscuring the small grey leaves, are a definite tonic to both. It is strong enough to thrive amongst small shrubs and herbaceous plants, as long as it has good drainage and full sun. For the rock garden, choose the cultivar 'Compactum', which is less invasive. The soft lemon-yellow flowers of 'Citrinum' are less harsh than those of *A. saxatile*. Trimming over the faded flower stems encourages bushiness and prolongs the life of the plants.

Amelanchier (Snowy Mespilus, June Berry) Nec./Pol. Shr. T. Deciduous.
ht: 3–3.5m *10–12ft* dist: 3.5–4.5m *12–15ft* Apr., full sun, semi-shade.
Few plants can have as many attributes as this easily grown, large, deciduous shrub or small tree.

In spring, the twiggy shoots are blanketed with erect clusters of snowy flowers. Each flower may be 2.5–3.5cm (1–1.5in) in diameter, with five, rather narrow, strap-shaped petals. The young leaves at this time are a coppery brown and provide an unusual and pleasant contrast with the flowers. The flowers may be followed by red or black fruits in the autumn, but these quickly succumb to the attention of birds, and are certainly not a prominent feature.

The leaves, however, are prominent and can provide breathtaking red-orange, orange-green, yellow-red combinations of colour – even on the same branch. Definitely one of the top five plants for autumn colour. No largish garden should be without its Amelanchier; not least because it must be one of the earliest sources of pollen. The genus is well represented in North America by some nine species, all of which are thought to be reasonably productive honey plants.

A. lamarkii. By far the most commonly grown species, although you might not think so if you are hunting through the average nursery for a specimen – in the past it has been widely but incorrectly known as *canadensis*, and old habits die hard. Other names frequently applied to it include *laevis* and *x grandiflora*. If you buy any of these you will in all probability end up with *lamarkii*! The leaves of this species are large, up to 10cm (4in) long by 5cm (2in) wide, and finely toothed. It has red berries.

I have a large 3.5 x 3.5m (12 x 12ft) specimen growing next to a dark green Lawson's Cypress, and the contrast in spring and again in autumn is beautiful.

'Rubescens' Flowers tinted pink.

Anchusa Nec.
Full sun.
The flowers of all the species and cultivars listed are brilliant gentian-blue and have five rounded petals, very slightly cupped, with a small white eye fringed with short hairs that protect the nectar from rain and short-tongued insects, but not from the honey bee. The leaves are narrow and very rough to the touch. Not the same colour as a cat's tongue, but much the same feel!

A. azurea 'Loddon Royalist' H. ht: 1m *3ft* dist: 60cm *2ft* Jun.–Sep. A fabulous plant with a long much-branched flower spike, all parts of which are bristly and rough to the touch.

The root systems of the perennial types are very fleshy and easily damaged, so try to buy container-grown plants; and if you have to move them, do so straight after flowering, while the soil is still warm, so that damaged parts heal quickly.

'Morning Glory' H. ht: 1.25–1.5m *4–5ft* dist: 75–90cm *2.5–3ft* Jun.–Sep. Deeper blue flowers.

A. capensis 'Blue Angel' A(h). ht: 23cm *9in* dist: 23cm *9in* Jun.–Nov. A less elegant form than its taller relatives, but with just as many flowers.

'Blue Bird' A(h). ht: 30cm *12in* dist: 23cm *9in* Jun.–Nov. Just a bit larger than 'Blue Angel'. There are now pink cultivars available.

A. officinalis (alkanet). A wild flower but well established in some gardens, it is a joy to all bees and many other insects. Flowering throughout the summer, it continues to provide both nectar and pollen at times when there is little else about.

Anemone (Windflower) Pol.
Full sun, semi-shade.
There is far more to this interesting genus of largely bulbous or rhizomatous plants than is to be seen in florists' windows. There are many European species, some dwarf, and some of the very best of all herbaceous plants in *A. x hybrida* and its cultivars. Anemones are easily grown, and the bulk of them flower from early to late spring, providing large amounts of pollen at a time

when few other sources may be available. Anemones have no nectaries. The flowers, which are normally carried singly, have a whorl of three leaves some way beneath them, and are parsley-like and attractive (in most species) long after the flowers are over.

A. blanda B./C. ht: 10cm *4in* dist: 7.5–10cm *3–4in* Mar.–Apr. The species has 3.5–5cm (1.5–2in) white-eyed, star-like, pale-blue flowers, but there are also cultivars with pink, red and purple flowers. Best planted in August or September, 7.5–10cm (3–4in) deep.

A. apenina B./C. ht: 12.5cm *5in* dist: 7.5–10cm *3–4in* Mar.–May. Very similar to *blanda*, but longer flowering and also ideal for naturalising in short grass. Both are charming dwarf plants for the rock garden, or at the front of a tree, shrub or herbaceous border.

A. coronaria (Poppy Anemone) B./C. ht: 25–30cm *10–12in* dist: 7.5–10cm *3–4in* Mar.–Oct. This is one of the parents from which the florists' strains such as 'St Brigid' and 'De Caen' were bred. There are now several named cultivars of these available in a wide range of bold, gaudy colours. The petals are

Anemone blanda. The pale-blue flowers are the *atrocoerulea* strain. There are pink, red and purple cultivars

Anemone apenina. A perfect bee friendly plant for borders, bases and rock gardens

rounded and only eight in number, as compared to, say, *blanda*, which may have up to twenty. The pollen is a slatey blue-grey colour. They are not reliably hardy, so unless you are prepared to protect your plants with cloches (and this is quite commonly done for autumn-planted tubers), plant only in late spring and summer to give a succession of flowers throughout mid-summer and autumn. Plant the tubers 5cm (2in) deep.

x hybrida H. Aug.–Nov. The nomenclature of this superb late-flowering group of herbaceous plants is much confused, at least as far as the poor gardener is concerned, for although *x hybrida* is the name now officially used, the plants are still frequently sold under their original species names: *hupehensis* and *japonica*, or even a combination of both: *hupehensis japonica*. The name *x hybrida* is in fact now given to crosses between the two species. The 6.5–7.5cm (2.5–3in) flowers, with their rounded satiny petals, are quite exquisite in form and texture. They are not carried singly as in other species, but in erect long-flowering compound heads that display buds and flowers beautifully. All have large central bosses of yellow-tipped stamens. The leaves are also bold, trifoliate with unequal lobes – with nothing parsley-like about

Anemone x hybrida a cross between *hupehensis* and *japonica*, the round satin-textured petals are not carried singly but in erect long-flowering heads displaying buds and flowers

them. There are several double and semi-double cultivars, so do make sure you buy what you want.

'Bressingham Glow' ht: 60cm *2ft* dist: 45cm *18in*. Deep-pink flowers.

'Honorine Jobert' ht: 1.25m *4ft* dist: 60–90cm *2–3ft*. Pure-white flowers.

'Kriemhilde' ht: 90cm *3ft* dist: 60cm *2ft*. Rose-pink flowers. I have this cultivar in the herbaceous border, where it looks very showy against holly, but any other dark background would do as well.

A. nemerosa (Wood Anemone) ht: 10cm *4in* dist: 7.5–10cm *3–4in* Mar.–May. The charming wood anemone, with its pink-flushed, white or pale blue, star-like, nodding flowers, has very catholic tastes regarding soil and site. In spite of its innocent looks, this is a very poisonous plant (not to bees), and its sap will also cause skin blistering.

Unlike *x hybrida*, which is fibrous rooted, and the other species listed which

Anemone nemorosa Wood Anemone

are tuberous, *nemerosa* is rhizomatous. Plant new rhizomes quickly (to prevent drying out) to a depth of 5cm (2in).

Anthemis Nec./Pol. H. Jun.–Sep. Evergreen.
Just one of the enormous family of plants with composite flowers, like daisies and dandelions, which all bees find so attractive and rewarding. The leaves of

all species are rather feathery and much divided, with a typical chamomile-like fragrance when crushed. This combination of leaves and flowers makes a rather handsome plant.

A. cupaniana ht: 15cm *6in* dist: 60–90cm *2–3ft* full sun, semi-shade. Forms great spreading mats of silver foliage topped with 5cm (2in) white flowers with a yellow eye. An ideal plant for a dry area where space is not at a premium.

A. sancti-johannis ht: 45cm *18in* dist: 30–45cm *12–18in* full sun. Flowers of bright orange, leaves hairy and grey.

A. tinctoria x 'Grallagh Gold' (Ox-Eye Chamomile) ht: 75cm *2.5ft* dist: 60cm *2ft* full sun. Somewhat deeper orange than *sancti-johannis.*

'Wargrave' Pale lemon-yellow flowers.

Arabis Nec./Pol.
Full sun, semi-shade.
Mostly rather dwarf-tufted or mat-forming perennials with basal rosettes of oval or lance-shaped leaves. The short flowering stems, which also bear leaves, are topped with clusters of rounded or flat-topped flowers, which may be white or even deep red-purple, depending on the cultivar. Like most crucifers, this plant provides nectar and pollen and is very attractive to the honey bee. As it flowers so early in the season it is a very useful plant in the spring build-up of honey bee colonies. The four petals are divided to the base, and are 'held' in place by the sepals. Nectar collects in copious amounts at the base of the sepals and petals.

A. albida 'Rosabella' ht: 10cm *4in* dist: 23cm *9in* Mar.–Jun. Fragrant pale-pink flowers, leaves grey-green.

'Coccinea' ht 10cm *4in.* Flowers a deeper red.

A. blepharophylla 'Spring Charm' ht: 10cm *4in* dist: 23cm *9in* Mar.–Jun. Very showy, fragrant and intense carmine flowers very nearly 2.5cm (1in) across; leaves green, somewhat rough. The sepals are distinctly boat-shaped and take on a good deal of the flower colouration. Although a native of California, this species is, in my experience, completely hardy in cooler areas such as Britain. Try it for a change in your spring bedding display instead of or with Bellis or Myosotis.

A. ferdinandi-coburgii 'Variegata' ht: 12.5cm *5in* dist: 30–46cm *12–15in* Apr.–Jun. A really awful name for a first-class rock-garden or edging plant.

The small flowers are white, as are the sepals, with occasional green markings. The bluntly pointed leaves are up to 4cm (1.5in) long, with wide irregular marginal variegation which often turns deep pink in winter. Runners are freely produced and root easily on contact with the soil. An excellent ground-cover plant that associates well with spring-flowering bulbs such as Chionodoxa, Muscari and Scilla.

Armeria (Thrift, Sea Pink) Nec./Pol.
Salt tol., full sun.
Seen growing wild in coastal or mountain areas, the tight hummocks of dark-green grass-like foliage of the thrifts could easily be mistaken for the sheep-mown grass with which they so happily combine. But when in flower there is no mistaking this superb little plant with its iron constitution.

The tight clusters of flower buds appear in spring. The flower stalks quickly elongate and the small, five-petalled, tubular flowers open, forming a dense, almost spherical, head of flowers. The bees visit the flowers in great numbers, and since there can be several hundred individual flowers in just one square foot the 'grazing' is good.

A. juniperfolio syn. *cespitosa* ht: 7.5cm *3in* dist: 15cm *6in* Apr.–May. Where space is really restricted, or you have a genuine rock garden or scree bed, one of the several cultivars of this tight pincushion-like plant with its almost stalkless flowers is ideal. The cultivar 'Bevans' has deep-rose flowers, 'Deep Form' has pale-pink flowers and the tightest growth habit of the whole genus.

A. maritima ht: 20cm *8in* dist: 23cm *9in* May–Jul. The flower heads are almost 2.5cm (1in) across. The cultivar 'Alba' has white flowers, 'Vindictive' is deep pink.

✓ **Aster** Nec./Pol. H.
Full sun.
The name Aster comes from the Greek word for star, and this is an apt description of the flowers, particularly the single-flowered cultivars, although even the doubles open up eventually to give access to the bees. Most members of the daisy family are highly attractive to bees and provide nectar and pollen in good quantity. The late-flowering Michaelmas daisies have the added advantage of coming into flower when there is very little bee forage, and colonies are needing to collect fresh pollen to add to their winter store of protein. Not only is pollen stored in the cells at this time of year, but the bees are also storing protein within their bodies, in an organ called the fatbody, which helps them survive the winter and reduces the ill effects of some diseases, such a nosema, a protozoan gut parasite. To the honey bee, any income of fresh food in autumn is very valuable, and the beekeeper-gardener should remember this when planning his garden.

Asters are a large and varied genus of plants perhaps characterised best by the Michaelmas daisies, known to most gardeners for their lax growth habits, late flowers and susceptibility to mildew; a reputation largely undeserved if a careful selection is made. There are also some beautiful dwarf spring/summer-flowering species and cultivars, and these are very suitable for the rock garden.

A. alpinus ht: 15–23cm *6–9in* dist: 15–23cm *6–9in* May–Jul. There can be few greater pleasures for the gardener than collecting seed in the wild, raising the plants and awaiting with eager anticipation the first flowers. My own plants were raised from seed collected on a walking holiday in the Maritime Alps, and it is a great pleasure when the first lilac-blue flowers open in spring. The single flowers are 4–5cm (1.5–2in) across, and their large, flat, yellow centres are packed with florets. The leaves are mostly basal and spoon-shaped. White and pink forms are frequently to be seen in gardens – as indeed they are in the wild.

A. tongolensis 'Napsbury' ht: 23cm *9in* dist: 23cm *9in* Jun.–Jul. A mat-forming cultivar displaying purple-blue flowers with orange centres. Often seen in cultivation as *yunnanensis* 'Napsbury'.

Michaelmas daisies are, strictly speaking, cultivars of the *novae-belgii* group, but all the species and cultivars described below also commonly bear this name. The flowers are borne in erect terminal clusters varying in size from 4–8cm (1.5–3in), and the leaves are narrow in relation to their length.

Many of the older types were tall and prone to collapse at around flowering time, making staking an essential operation. The newer introductions have often been selected for their more dwarf characteristics, making them easier to manage; so, unless you enjoy staking and tying, or really want tall plants, choose from the newer types listed here.

A. amellus 'Brilliant' ht: 60cm *2ft* dist: 45–60cm *1.5–2ft* Aug.–Oct. Large bright-pink flowers.

'Violet Queen' ht: 60cm *2ft* dist: 45–60cm *1.5–2ft* Aug.–Oct. Violet flowers.

A. dumosus 'Lady in Blue' ht: 30m *12in* dist: 30cm *12in* Sep.–Oct. Semi-double lavender-blue flowers. Susceptible to mildew.

A. x frikartii 'Monch' ht: 60–75cm *2–2.5ft* dist: 45–60cm *1.5–2ft* Jul.–Oct. Large 5cm (2in) rich lavender-blue flowers, centre yellow-orange.

A. novae-belgii ht: 30cm *1ft* dist: 23–30cm *9–12in* Sep.–Oct. All cultivars are susceptible to mildew.

'Little Pink Beauty' Semi-double flowers.

'Snowsprite' Both this and the cultivar above have flowers which contrast well with the very dark-green foliage.

A. sedifolius nanus syn. *acris* ht: 60cm *2ft* dist: 45cm *18in* Sep.–Oct. Masses of small violet-blue flowers with few petals. Leaves small and pale green, smelling of carrot when bruised.

A. thomsonii nana ht: 30cm *12in* Jul.–Oct. Pale-blue flowers.

Some taller-growing cultivars that would help to extend the colour range are: *novae angliae* 'Alma Potschke' Cerise, semi-double, and 'Harrington's Pink' Salmon; *novae belgii* 'Ernest Ballard' Crimson.

✓   **Aubrieta** (Aubretia) Nec./Pol. H.
ht: 15cm *6in* dist: 45–60 cm *1.5–2ft* Mar.–May, full sun, semi-shade.
A single plant will, over two or three years, cover a square metre (yard) of soil or cascade over a similar area of wall, and when smothered with its small blue, purple or white flowers it would be difficult to imagine a more pleasing sight. The plants are usually only a few inches high, but will 'clamber up' to a height of 60cm (2ft) or so if taller plants nearby provide competition. They are equally at home in sunny south-facing crevices on walls or rock gardens with virtually no soil or moisture and a high pH, as they are in richer soils with a low pH and a northerly aspect. The foliage is an unremarkable grey-green. The bees will prefer those plants in full sun. They will, however, work the flowers at any time when the air temperature is high enough to make flight possible, because Aubretia is another member of the crucifer family, and thus very attractive to honey bees.

    As soon as the flowers are over, clip off the old flower stalks with shears. This prevents the plants looking untidy and encourages new growth from the base of the plant. Cuttings taken from these new shoots will root easily in May or June.

    The matted habit of Aubrieta encourages slugs and snails, and although the plants do not appear to suffer damage themselves, they do provide bases for attacks on other susceptible plants. Use slug pellets every few weeks or traps and barriers, especially in spring and autumn. Pink and red seed-raised plants are commonly available in garden centres.

A. deltoidea 'Dr Mules' Deep violet-blue, probably the most commonly grown variety.

'Variegata' Less vigorous and a tidier grower than the green-leaved types. The marginal variegation makes a very pretty contrast with the violet-blue flowers. A fine garden plant.

Berberis (Barberry) Nec./Pol. Shr.
Full sun, semi-shade.

The popularity and variability of these splendid shrubs, which range in height from 30cm to well over 3m (1ft–10ft), cannot be denied. Garden centres carry a wide range, and specialist nurseries may stock 150 or more. All the species are very attractive to honey bees, and large shrubs will be abuzz with bees when in flower, some collecting the greenish-yellow pollen, others the abundant, good-quality nectar.

The drooping clusters of individual flowers appear in spring along the entire length of either stiffly erect or gently arching branches. The evergreen types generally have showier flowers then the deciduous ones, and these may be yellow, orange or orange-red, rarely exceeding 8mm (0.33in) in diameter, and cup-and-saucer shaped. There are six sepals, and all the flower parts are of the same colour. The stamens are sensitive to touch, and when bees probe for the nectar held in six separate nectaries at the base of the petals, pollen is 'dabbed' on the bee's proboscis, thus ensuring cross-pollination when another flower is visited.

Berberis usually flower so freely that the very condensed side shoots (which appear as single leaves or rosettes) from which the flowers arise, may be obscured. Likewise the not infrequently vicious spines, which may be up to 7.5cm (3in) long – the epithet 'prickle' or 'thorn' simply does not do them full justice! The spines are usually in threes (although there may be two other rudimentary ones), and form a T shape, joining the stem at the head of the T.

The clusters of berries start to appear in early autumn, and in some species and cultivars disappear very quickly, due to the depredations of blackbirds in particular, before any real colouration is noticeable. *B. darwinii* is particularly susceptible to these attacks, even though one might think its small dark purple-black berries would not appear as attractive to birds as the beautiful eye-catching, coral-red, translucent berries of *B. wilsoniae*. Yet this is one of the last to be stripped by birds. Beauty is, in this case, obviously more than skin deep! The fruits rarely exceed 6mm (0.25in) in diameter, and may be spherical or oval. Leaf shapes vary from the long narrow ones of *B. x stenophylla* to the elliptic shape of *B. candidula*. The autumn colours of the deciduous species and cultivars can be stunning, with brilliant reds and oranges predominating, many of the evergreens are a perfect foil for the bright flowers of a range of other plants.

A fair number of the Berberis are vigorous growers and will quickly smother other less strongly growing neighbours, so unless you have plenty of space, limit your choice to the less vigorous types. Most of the deciduous types are tolerant of windy exposed situations, and are useful for hedging or as a first line of defence for more delicate subjects.

B. buxifolia 'Nana' ht: 60cm *2ft* dist: 45cm *18in* Apr.–May. A slow-growing, mound-forming plant with purple berries in autumn.

Opposite: *B. x lologensis*, a natural hybrid between *B. darwinii* and *B. linearifolia*

B. x carminea 'Buccaneer' ht: 1.5m *5ft* dist: 1.25m *4ft* Jun.–Jul. The smallish leaves colour well in autumn, and are complemented by the large deep-red berries which are carried well into the winter.

B. candidula ht: 60cm *2ft* dist: 45cm *18in* May–Jun. Densely mounded growth habit, with dark-green leaves, that are silver-grey beneath. Flowers are bright yellow, followed by purplish fruits in autumn.

B. darwinii ht: 2.25m *7ft* dist: 1.5m *5ft* Apr.–May. With its small glossy, holly-like leaves and scented orange-yellow flowers, this is a deservedly popular species. The purple berries are usually taken early by birds.

B. gagnepainii ht: 2m *6ft* dist: 1.25m *4ft* May–Jun. The dark-green leaves, which are normally lance-shaped, may be up to 10cm (4in) long. The pale yellow flowers are invariably followed by masses of blackish berries with a purple bloom.

B. julianae ht: 2.75m *9ft* dist: 2–2.25m *6–7ft* May. A strong, dense grower, the stems heavily spined. The young spiny leaves are coppery at first, and some of the older leaves frequently turn reddish in autumn. The pale yellow, scented flowers are followed by oval black fruits, with a blue bloom.

B. linearifolia 'Orange King' ht: 2.25m *7ft* dist: 1.25–1.5m *4–5ft* Apr.–May. The stiffly erect form of this cultivar would discourage many from wanting it in their own garden – that is, until they have seen the flowers. These are a rich orange and have the deepest colouration of any of the Berberis. There may occasionally be the bonus of a second, but less vigorous, flowering season in the autumn. The berries are black with a purple bloom, the leaves are dark green above and grey beneath. Completely hardy.

B. x stenophylla ht: 2.75m *9ft* dist: 2.25–2.75m *7–9ft* Apr.–May. A big garden will be required to give this marvellous plant full rein. Grown as a specimen it will grow wider than it is high, its arching branches literally wreathed with the scented bright orange-yellow flowers, the dark-green linear leaves seemingly nowhere in evidence. The black berries are not such an impressive spectacle. For those with less space, try one of the dwarfer forms of *x stenophylla* listed below.

'Crawley Gem' ht: 1m *3ft* dist: 60cm *2ft* May. Flowers orange-red, berries black.

'Corallina Compacta' ht: 45cm *18in* dist: 30–45cm *12–18in* May–Jun. A neat little plant with tight clusters of small matt green leaves contrasting well with its coral-red flower buds, which open to a deep yellow.

'Semperflorens' ht: 1m *3ft* dist: 60cm *2ft* May–Jun. This cultivar has a longer flowering season than the type, and this should endear it to beekeepers.

The bulk of the deciduous Berberis comes from the single genus *thunbergii*, which has some very diverse and worthy cultivars to its name, all of which flower in April–May, and have small rounded leaves which colour well in autumn.

B. thunbergii 'Atropurpurea' ht: 1.5m *5ft* dist: 1.25m *4ft*. This handsome and graceful shrub is seen less frequently now that the more strongly coloured (and to my mind more vulgar) and stiffly erect cultivars such as 'Red Chief' and 'Red Pillar' are the darlings of the garden centres. In my own garden the purplish leaves contrast well with the yellow stonecrop which has taken over the ground beneath, where little else will grow. The flowers are a pale orange and are followed by glistening bright-red oval berries, rather profusely borne. For those with less space the dwarf form 'Atropurpurea Nana' is a very acceptable substitute.

'Aurea' ht: 1m *3ft* dist: 60cm *2ft*. Lovely lemon yellow-green foliage, but it does need sun for the foliage to colour well, and shelter to avoid scorching. Bright-red berries in autumn.

'Harlequin' ht: 1.5m *5ft* dist: 1.25m *4ft*. A not unattractive and very popular pink-leaved form with white splashes; more showy than the older cultivar 'Rose Glow'. Red berries in autumn.

B. wilsoniae ht: 1.25m *4ft* dist: 1.25m *4ft*. No-one would grow this species for its form, leaf colour or pale yellow flowers alone; but the brilliant translucent coral-red berries produced in tight clusters all along the branches that hang on well into the winter give it, for me, an edge over any of the other Berberis. Nothing could look more deliciously edible than the fruits of this species. The sea-green leaves also give good autumn colour.

Bergenia Pol. H.
Mar.–May, full sun, semi-shade.
Easily grown, large shiny-leaved evergreens, with good autumn leaf colouration and showy 12–20mm (0.5–0.75in) diameter flowers of pink, or red, but also white and pale primrose.

Bergenias, with their clumps of broadly ovate leaves up to 30cm (1ft) long, produced from a compact semi-woody rootstock, have few equals as good, all-round garden plants.

Marvellously versatile in their own right, they also blend so well with other plant forms that they are indispensable in this respect alone.

The thick-stemmed, frequently wine-coloured flower stems carry bell-shaped flowers, the centres of which are packed with a ring of yellow-tipped stamens, the pollen from which is avidly collected.

B. cordifolia ht: 45cm *18in* dist: 45cm *18in*. Several different coloured forms of this species are seen in cultivation, the most common of which has flowers of a lovely silvery-pink, which last well on into summer.

B. purpurascens 'Ballawley' ht: 60cm *2ft* dist: 60cm *2ft*. Very large leaves which turn a beautiful dull pinky-red in autumn.

'Evening Glow' ht: 45cm *18in* dist: 45cm *18in*. Neat wavy-edged, rounded leaves which colour maroon to plum-red in winter. Flowers semi-double and rose-red, mainly in spring but intermittently through the summer as well. This cultivar would probably be most people's first choice because of the boldness of its leaves and excellent winter leaf colouration.

Borago officinalis (Borage) Nec./Pol. A(h).   ✓
ht: 30–45cm *12–18in* dist: 45–60cm *1.5–2ft* Apr.–Oct, full sun, semi-shade.
Covered as it is in short stiff hairs, this plant is as unpleasant to handle as an unshaven chin! But the vivid gentian-blue flowers carried in nodding clusters more than compensate for this – they are fabulous. The dark-green calyx points project between the pointed petal lobes, creating the effect of a ten-pointed star. The base of each petal is a pale blue and projects upwards slightly, forming, with the ring of five dark-purplish anthers, a 'reservoir' in which nectar accumulates. The leaves may be up to 20cm (8in) long.
   Borage self-seeds quite happily, even in relatively poor soils, and not infrequently produces a few variegated forms which are even more handsome than the type. It is also occasionally grown as an agricultural crop on a field scale. Beekeepers who have had bees on these fields are very variable in their assessment of its value as a honey producer, but at times it does produce a good nectar flow.

Buddleia Nec. Shr.
Dry, full sun.
Easily grown shrubs thriving under the driest soil conditions, but most species and cultivars are rather large for the small garden. The flower tubes are up to 8–10mm (3–4in) long, and you might think it impossible for the bees to reach the nectar, but extract it they do, the nectar building up in the narrow corolla tubes to allow this.

B. alternifolia ht: 3.5m *12ft* dist: 2.5–3m *8–10ft* Jun.–Jul. The slender arching branches bear clusters of sweetly scented lilac flowers along their entire

B. alternifolia, beautiful in colour, shape and scent

length in early summer. The leaves are grey-green and lance-shaped, up to 10cm (4in) long. A most elegant and graceful shrub.

B. davidii (Butterfly Bush) ht: 2.5–3.5m *8–12ft* dist: 2.5–3m *8–10ft* Jul.–Sep. A large gaunt shrub with gently arching flower spikes up to 60cm (2ft) long. The individual flowers are legion and have a conspicuous orange eye, the very pleasant fragrance attracting butterflies and bees in profusion. The leaves are long and narrow, with fine forward-pointing teeth, dark green above and conspicuously grey beneath. If left unpruned, the bushes quickly become untidy and the flowers progressively smaller. To prevent this, prune hard back annually in March to within a few buds of the previous season's growth.

'Black Knight' Deep-violet flowers.

'Fascination' Bright pink flowers.

B. globosa, Orange Ball Tree

'Harlequin' The red-purple flowers contrast nicely with the attractively varie-gated leaves. A fine plant, with the added bonus that it is less vigorous than its green brethren.

'Royal Red' Very striking deep red-purple flowers.

'White Cloud' White flowers.

B. globosa (Orange Ball Tree) Ht: 2.5–3.5m *8–12ft* dist: 2.5–3m *8–10ft* May–Jun. When it flowers well, *globosa* is a striking plant, but its irregular performances in this respect, coupled with its large size, have kept it from being grown in most private gardens. The terminal clusters of 2.5cm (1in) orange balls are composed of many small flowers with much shorter corolla tubes than other species, affording bees ease of access to the nectar. The long leaves have a 'crinkly' surface and are greyish-green above, grey beneath. Evergreen in mild districts, deciduous in cold ones.

B. davidii Butterfly Bush

Calluna vulgaris (Ling or Heather) Nec./Pol. Shr.
ht: 45cm *18in* dist: 30cm *12in*
Jul.–Nov., acid, full sun.
This straggly dwarf evergreen plant covers very many thousands of acres of moorland areas throughout Britain and Europe. Rounded or rocky hills covered with purplish pink flowers in August and September are a sight that once seen, is never forgotten. Walking across the springy stems is tiring, but these same stems make a very comfortable seat, and from this close range some variability of flower colour, from white through pink to purple, can clearly be observed. Hopefully, when grown in the private garden, there will be sufficient shelter for the bees to work the flowers in late summer – this is not always the case on windy moorland areas. The small flowers are actually shorter than the calyx, which at under 6mm (0.25inch) long – and wide – is more ornamental

Bees enjoying *B. globosa*, the Orange Ball Tree

and consists of four narrowly oval sepals. The one-sided flower spike may be up to 30cm (12in) long. The dead flowers will persist through the winter and are not unattractive.

Individual cultivars flower over about a two-month period between July and November. Most Callunas are now pot-grown, so if you are unsure if a plant has single or double flowers, check it out at the nursery or garden centre when in flower, and then make your purchase. Those cultivars with coloured foliage usually flower freely, but before getting carried away, as inevitably you will be if you are warmed by their rich colours on winter days, remember that an acid soil is a must. To help prevent the plants taking on their characteristic straggly appearance, clip the dead flower spikes in spring just before new growth commences. The much-branched stems are densely covered with small overlapping leaves in four rows, giving a distinct quadrangular outline.

A cultivar of *C. vulgaris*. Callunas are extremely popular garden plants, but they must have an acid soil

Ling honey has been variously described as 'glorious', 'unusual' and 'strong flavoured'. It is also almost unique, there being only three other plants in the world which produce a similar honey. Heather honey, as it is more commonly called, is a jelly, does not crystallise and is somewhat bitter in flavour, rather than sweet. The bouquet is distinctive and can sometimes be detected in a sample of honey which has no visible evidence of containing heather honey. Honey from the Erica heathers is different, and does not gel, and it is usually called bell heather honey.

'Alba Aurea' Aug.–Sep. A white-flowered form which has yellow-tipped foliage.

'Alportii Praecox' Flowers crimson, borne early July/August.

'Blazeaway' Aug.–Sep. Flowers lilac-mauve, the green foliage changing to a rich red-bronze in winter. Stunning.

'Hibernica' Oct.–Nov. Flowers of mauve, very freely borne and often obscuring the foliage of this very compact form.

'Pallida' Aug.–Sep. Flowers of pale pink.

'Serlei Aurea' Oct.–Nov. Flowers white in long racemes, with golden foliage.

Caltha palustris (Marsh Marigold/King-cups) Nec./Pol. H.
ht: 30cm *12in* dist: 45cm *18in*
Mar.–Jun., wet, full sun, semi-shade.
Before the days of the agricultural rip out hedges and drain every spare corner of land' brigade in Britain, and similar movements in some parts of Europe, the marsh marigold reigned supreme in just about every marshy corner, along with the cuckoo pint, marsh orchid and primrose. They were all part of the country scene, and it is sad that they are all now so diminished in number. However, there are still good populations in marshy places, and even at the edge of fast-flowing streams, where there may be quite marked changes in water-level.

The flowers have five–eight rounded petals and are borne in lax leafy clusters on semi-erect hollow stems arising from a stout creeping rhizome. As with most buttercup-like plants, the flowers glisten in strong light, and groups of marsh marigolds provide a brilliant splash of gold in wet spring meadows. The rounded leaves are also shiny, and up to 10cm (4in) in length. Honey bees and bumble-bees work the golden flowers with great relish, taking away nectar and large loads of bright-yellow pollen. They often use the lowest leaves as landing sites when collecting water. Caltha must have a very moist or boggy soil, and will even thrive under water to a maximum depth of 23cm (9in).

'Alba' is a white form with a yellow centre, insipid in comparison with the species, but appealing to some.

Campanula (Bell Flower) Nec./Pol.   ✓
Full sun, semi-shade.
Surely one of the most versatile, easily grown and free-flowering of all herbaceous and alpine plants. Although predominantly blue, you can find white, pink and pale-yellow flowered species. All are attractive to bees, the larger forms providing a bountiful source of pollen.

The generic name (which the common name also reflects) is in fact a description of the flower shape. These may be shallowly bell-shaped or more tubular, with only minimal reflexing of the five petals. The alpine types in particular bear their erect or nodding flowers on such delicate stems that the slightest breeze will set them prettily in motion.

CAMPANULA: HERBACEOUS AND BIENNIAL TYPES

Many of these more robust species and cultivars are suitable not only for herbaceous borders but for mixed borders, where they will compete quite strongly for space. The leaves are generally toothed and lance-shaped with rounded bases.

C. x burghaltii H. ht: 45cm *18in* dist: 30cm *1ft* Jun. and Sep. The deep-purple, 7.5cm (3in) long flower buds open to pale blue.

C. glomerata (Clustered Bell Flower) H. ht: 45cm *18in* dist: 60cm *2ft* Jun.–Sep. A rather stiffly erect plant with rough leaves, carrying its violet-purple, 2.5–5cm (1–2in) star-like flowers in tight -terminal clusters. Bold and handsome, if rather less graceful than other species. A white-flowered form is available.

C. lactiflora H. ht: 1.5m *5ft* dist: 1m *3ft* Jul.–Sep. Rather open flowers 2.5cm (1in) or so wide, in crowded heads of palest blue.

'Alba' White flowers.

'Prichard's Variety' Deep violet-blue flowers.

C. latifolia H. ht: 1.25m *4ft* dist: 60cm *2ft* Jun.–Jul. Multi-directional, 5cm (2in) bell-shaped flowers, powder blue, carried in elegantly tapered spikes. The white form 'Alba' is slightly less vigorous.

'Gloaming' Very pale blue.

C. medium (Canterbury Bell) Bien. ht: 45cm *18in* dist: 30cm *1ft* May–Jul. Bells 5cm (2in) long, of blue, pink or white. The aptly named Cup and Saucer types are now the most commonly seen and Canterbury Bells have returned to gardens once again. With their indefinable cottage-garden feel they look perfect set among a jumble of other plants.

C. poscharskyana H. ht: 30cm *1ft* dist: 60cm *2ft* May–Sep. Lavender-blue 2.5cm (1in) star-shaped flowers. It spreads quickly.

Castanea sativa (Sweet or Spanish Chestnut) Nec./Pol. T.
ht: 27–30m *90–100ft*
Jul., acid, full sun.
Far too large in its maturity for any but the biggest garden, but a common enough tree on neutral or acid soils in warmer parts of Europe and Britain. It is sometimes 'cropped' as a coppice tree, for which its growth habit and wood

quality is ideally suited. It is not normally regarded as a fast grower, but when coppiced there are few other trees that can keep pace with it. The sweet chestnut is the longest-lived of all deciduous trees, and develops a deeply fissured bark that spirals around the trunk.

The handsome glossy saw-toothed leaves are conspicuously veined and may be up to 25cm (10in) long and 8.5cm (3in) wide. They are very persistent even after they fall in autumn, so persistent in fact that in parts of Europe they are used as 'baking plates' and 'wraps' for brioches.

The male and female flowers are borne on separate catkins in the leaf axils of the young shoots, the males being up to 23cm (9in) in length. Although the individual, pale yellow-green catkins are inconspicuous, their sheer volume turns the tree into a distinct and showy sight.

Heavy crops of the brown shiny chestnuts are rarely produced in Britain, unless there is a hot dry summer (an all too infrequent occurrence). Bees work the trees very heavily for pollen, which is very small in size and consequently often found in some quantity in honey. In warm weather there is a good nectar flow, and this is produced in quantity in warmer areas such as Spain. The prickly green cases that enclose the chestnuts need no description – for who has not suffered a few pricks trying to extract the nuts. Pigs, however, seem to have little or no such trouble, and in part of Corsica, where wild pigs still abound, the flavour of their meat testifies to this. The cultivar 'Marron De Lyon' is regarded as the best fruiting cultivar.

Ceanothus Nec./Pol. Shr.
Full sun.
The Californian lilacs are not the hardiest of shrubs, but once you have seen them in frothy full flower you will find it difficult to resist trying to grow them, albeit against a wall for protection. Take a few cuttings each summer as an insurance policy against a hard winter's frosts.

The flower spikes are packed with tiny, usually blue, flowers. From between the incurving sepals emerge the five ladle-like petals, each with one yellow-tipped stamen. The stigma emerges from the centre of the calyx. The individual flower stalks take on the colour of the flower, adding considerably to the overall effect, as do the glossy leaves, particularly of the evergreen types.

Most are lime tolerant, but will not do well on shallow chalky soils. The evergreen species are less tolerant of salt spray than their deciduous counterparts. Only species or cultivars that are regarded as reasonably hardy are listed below, but you may feel inclined to try others.

EVERGREENS

'Autumnal Blue' ht: 2m *6ft* dist: 1.25–1.5m *4–5ft* May–Sep. Possibly the hardiest of the evergreen cultivars. Flowers medium blue in spikes, about 9cm (3in) long.

'Southmead' ht: 2m *6ft* dist: 1.25–1.5m *4–5ft* May. Has a dense habit of growth, with bright-blue flowers.

C. thrysiflorus ht: 2.5–3m *8–10ft* dist: 2–2.5m *6–7ft* May–Jun. Rich blue flowers borne in early summer. A large plant that will eventually reach 6m (20ft) or more. The mound-forming *repens* – a form of *thrysiflorus* – grows to only about 45cm (18in), making it more suitable for the smaller garden.

DECIDUOUS

'Gloire de Versailles' ht: 2m *6ft* dist: 1.25–1.5m *4–5ft* Jul.–Sep., salt tol. By far the most widely grown cultivar, and deservedly so. Very large flower spikes of light blue.

'Marie Simon' ht: 2m *6ft* dist: 1.25–1.5m *4–5ft* Jul.–Sep., salt tol. Pink flowers.

'Perle Rose' ht: 2m *6ft* dist: 1.25–1.5m *4–5ft* Jul.–Sep., salt tol. A paler pink than 'Marie Simon'.

'Topaz' ht: 2m *6ft* dist: 1.25–1.5m *4–5ft* Jul.–Sep., salt tol. Bright-blue flowers.

✔ **Centaurea** Nec./Pol.
Full sun.
Handsome plants, not unlike de-prickled thistles. The rounded or oval 'heads' (from the top of which erupt the flowers) are made up of overlapping bracts which are prettily fringed, rather like eyelashes. In some species the dark spots on the bracts exude nectar, and honey bees can clearly be seen gently probing for this – even preferring unopened buds to those in full flower.

The individual florets of the flowers are tubular, with five shallow lobes, the outer ones usually much longer than the inner ones, sometimes making access to the nectar impossible for the bee.

There is a large number of native species (in Britain and Europe usually known as knapweeds or hardheads) that really are best left in the wild. Being late flowering, these plants have suffered particularly badly from verge mowing in the past, but are now making a comeback, especially on calcerous soils, where they thrive. The honey of knapweed is extremely strong in flavour, reminding me of cough mixture, and is useful when blending honey. Useful loads of white pollen are readily collected.

C. candidissima syn. *rutifolia* and *cineraria* First-class grey foliage plants usually grown as annuals, although they are in fact perennial. They are rather tender and only worth growing long-term in milder coastal districts, where they will produce flowers after their second growing season from seed. Do not attempt to divide up plants.

C. cyanus (Cornflower) A(h). A charming plant with grey strap-shaped leaves and 3cm (1.25in) dark-blue flowers. Many of the newer cultivars bred from *cyanus* are excellent in colour, range and form, but unfortunately have 'double' flowers which, from the bees' point of view, means a larger proportion of longer tubular ray-florets with inaccessible nectar sources.

C. cyanus Cornflower

'Polka Dot Mixed' ht: 45cm *18in* dist: 23cm *9in* Jun.–Oct. A superb mixture of white, pink, blue, red and mauve flowers up to 5cm (2in) in diameter.

C. hypocleuca 'John Coutts' H. ht: 60cm *2ft* dist: 45cm *18in* Jun.–Jul. Large 7.5cm (3in) pink flowers with a yellow eye and much divided grey-green leaves.

'Steenbergii' H. ht: 60cm *2ft* dist: 45cm *18in* Jul.–Sep. Crimson flowers with a white eye.

C. macrocephala H. ht: 1.25m *4ft* dist: 1m *3ft* Aug.–Oct. A quite distinct species with 9cm (3in) bright-yellow flower heads, and shiny, dark brown, papery bud-scales. Well worth growing.

C. montana H. ht: 60cm *2ft* dist: 45cm *18in* Jun.–Oct. The distinct dark-brown extra-floral nectaries are quite apparent on this species. The blue ray florets form a single rather sparse ring which accentuates the dull red centre, giving a most effective colour contrast. The winged stems, which bear lance-shaped to oval leaves, add the final touch to one of the best of all herbaceous plants. There are white, pink and red forms to choose from.

C. moschata (Sweet Sultan) A(h). ht: 45cm *18in* dist: 23cm *9in* Jun.–Sep. The 5cm (2in) fragrant flower heads of this species are rather more spikey than others, giving a powder-puff-like effect in yellow, pink, white, carmine and rose – irresistible!

Cercis siliquastrum Nec./Pol. T.
ht: 3–3.5m *10–12ft* dist: 3.5–4.5m *12–15ft*
May–Jun., full sun.
Most commonly known as the Judas Tree, this densely twiggy plant will form a small tree if encouraged, but left to its own devices it is much happier as a large rounded shrub. Given a warmer climate, however, it can easily reach 15m (50ft) or so. The small vivid, pinky-purple, pea-like flowers are borne in profusion on young and old branches alike, and also directly on the main trunks and branches, often before any leaves have been produced. For brightness of flower colour Cercis has few equals; there are unfortunately many poor seed-raised plants with weak flowering habits in cultivation.

The flowers, which are very attractive to bees, are followed by clusters of red-brown pods up to 10cm (4in) in length. There is a white form, 'Alba', and a much darker one, 'Bodnant', with deep-purple flowers. Although it will thrive on heavier soils, drainage must be good.

Chaenomeles Nec./Pol. Shr.
ht: 1.25–1.5m *4–5ft* dist: 1.25–1.5m *4–5ft*
Mar.–Jun., full sun, shade.

C. speciosa

You may have heard Chaenomeles referred to as quince, Cydonia or Japonica. Call it what you will, it is a deservedly popular shrub, with its long flowering season and attractive fruits borne on densely twiggy and thorny shoots.

The flowers, up to 4cm (1.5in) in diameter, are borne in tight clusters in the early spring and summer, and the bright-red and orange cultivars in particular make a warm sight on cold March days. Being a somewhat untidy grower, Chaenomeles is most often seen planted against a wall, where it is 'contained' by regular spur pruning. This includes cutting back all those side

Chaenomoles, also referred to as Cydonia or Japonica

shoots produced the previous summer to 5cm (2in) or so in February. This not only keeps the plants within bounds but also allows a clear view of the flowers. These are five-petalled and spoon-shaped, with numerous anthers making a conspicuous and attractive feature. Odd flowers can be found at just about any time of year. Grown as wall shrubs, an area of 7.5sq.m (9 x 9ft) will be covered without too much difficulty in four to five years.

After flowering, the aromatic, hard yellow quinces follow. These may be 5cm (2in) in diameter, but can be as large as 18cm (7in) in vigorous species such as *cathayensis*. In a mild winter the fruits will persist until spring. The finely toothed, rounded leaves vary in shape and have attractive reddish hues when young.

C. speciosa 'Moerloosii' The flowers are a delicate pink and white.

'

Nivalis' Pure-white flowers.

C x superba 'Crimson and Gold' Crimson petals with prominent golden anthers.

'Ball of Fire' Orangey-red flowers.

'Knapp Hill Scarlet' Bright orange-scarlet flowers freely produced.

Cheiranthus (Wallflower) Nec./Pol. Bien. H.   ✓
Salt tol., full sun.
For as long as anyone can remember, wallflowers were the gardeners' favourite for bedding out in autumn, when the summer bedding plants were over. This has now changed, and most of what would have been beds of wall-flowers are planted instead with plants that give autumn, winter and spring colour, such as winter-flowering pansies, polyanthus and daisies. This is not too difficult to understand, since the wallflower is a rather boring plant from October to April, but in April and May the display is superb and the flowers deliciously fragrant – a fragrance which will pervade the whole garden on warm still days.

   No wonder bees are attracted in large numbers. The four-petalled flowers are carried in terminal spikes which will go on flowering until June if allowed to do so, but are often replaced by the impatient gardener with Geraniums, Lobularia and Lobelia. Wallflowers are then usually treated as biennials, but they are perennial and several vegetatively propagated named cultivars are available.

C. x alionii syn. *Erysimum x alionii* ht: 30cm *12in* dist: 23–30cm *9–12in* Apr.–May. Botanically this plant is more correctly known as Erysimum (it has six nectaries instead of two as in Cheiranthus), but to most of us it is still known as the Siberian wallflower. The flowers are bright vibrant orange, and are borne in slightly rounded heads. Apricot and lemon-yellow cultivars are also available.

C. cheiri ht: 15–45cm *6–18in* dist: 15–30cm *6–12in* Apr.–May. The colour range is wide: 'Blood Red', 'Cloth of Gold', 'Primrose Monarch', 'Ruby Gem', 'Scarlet Bedder' and 'Ivory White', to name but a few. The more dwarf bedding cultivars are around 30–40cm (12–15in), and there are also the so-called Tom Thumb types at 15–23cm (6–9in).
   One of the two long-flowering, vegetatively propagated cultivars that is suitable for the herbaceous border, rock garden or dry wall crevice is 'Bowles Mauve' ht: 60cm *2ft* dist: 30–45m *12–18in* Apr.–Aug. Its rich, purple flowers are shown to advantage against the dark-green foliage. The other is 'Moonlight' ht: 15cm *6in* dist: 15cm *6in* Apr.–Aug. Lemon-yellow flowers.

Chionodoxa Nec./Pol. B./C.
ht: 15cm *6in* dist: 7.5cm *3in*
Feb.–Apr., full sun, semi-shade.
The English translation of this difficult name is 'Glory of the Snow', and how well named it is, standing up to severe frost, snow and gales without damage or the need to close up its pale blue and white flowers for protection, as many other plants do. They grow well in short grass and look particularly good at the edges of borders of spring-flowering shrubs such as Forsythia. They thrive and quickly colonise under a very wide range of conditions, compacted gravel drives and paths, or the bases of walls in sun or shade, being favoured locations.

Most of the species are less than 15cm (6in) in height, but can rise above this if they are grown through low ground cover such as Erica *herbacea*. What a contrast these two plants make, particularly when one of the dark red, winter/spring flowering cultivars is chosen, and how spoilt for choice are the bees that find these two plants growing together!

After flowering, copious quantities of seed are normally set, and these green to red 'marbles' (seed pods) cause the flower stem to collapse under their weight. The pods are not unattractive, and eventually will be responsible for new colonies of seedlings which will be produced close to the parent plant. Where more than one species is grown, hybridisation appears to occur freely, resulting in variable offspring. This may be one of the reasons why the nomenclature of this species, particularly in the bulb trade, is so confused. The bulbs should be planted 7cm (3in) deep, as soon as they become available in autumn.

C. luciliae Most of the bulbs sold bear this name, probably incorrectly. If you purchase them you will almost certainly get a robust 20–25cm (8–10in) flower spike bearing 6–10 blue flowers with largish white centres. Each flower will measure approximately 2.5cm (1in) across.

C. sardensis Smaller, earlier flowering and more dainty than *luciliae*, being only 12.5cm (5in) or so high, with up to a dozen 1cm (0.4in) flowers with a small white eye.

Choisya ternata (Mexican Orange Blossom) Pol. Shr.
ht: 1.5m *5ft* dist: 2m *6ft*
May–Jun. and Aug.–Sep., full sun, semi-shade.
A most handsome shrub with deep-green trifoliate leaves, each shiny leaflet up to 7.5cm (3in) in length and emitting a pungent odour when bruised.
The pure-white flowers, 3.5cm (1.5in) in diameter, have seven petals and these do not overlap, giving a propeller-like impression. The stalks of the stamens, which vary in number and length, are also pure white, tipped with yellow anthers which curve inwards slightly over the sceptre-like ovary. Beauty enough, but the wonderful fragrance, like orange blossom, is the crown to add to the sceptre.

Give it a sheltered spot, preferably close to a path or the house so the fragrance can be readily enjoyed. Choisya is hardy in most parts of Britain and western Europe, but it can be severely damaged or even killed during prolonged periods of severe frost; fortunately cuttings taken in August root easily.

Cirsium Nec./Pol. H.
ht: 1m *3ft* dist: 60cm *2ft*
Jun.–Sep.
Far and few are those that welcome thistles into their gardens, but they are attractive and interesting flowers, and in many cases, where the narrow flower tubes are short enough, produce a good supply of late-season nectar for the honey bee. Remember to remove the old flower heads before the seeds mature and float like 'thistle down' to every corner of your, and everyone else's garden. Less invasive are the cultivated types, of which only two species are usually seen, both of which have typical thistle-like leaves.

C. japonicum Flowers pink to purple, up to 5cm (2in) in diameter.

C. rivulare 'Atropurpureum' Flowers dull red-purple up to 3.5cm (1.5in) in diameter singly, or in terminal clusters on 'woolly' stems.

Although the Scottish thistle is actually an Onopordum, it is a really worthwhile plant of statuesque form. Up to 1.8m (6ft) high, with its winged spiny grey leaves and flower stems, there is no grander plant. For sheer impact it rates alongside the Himalayan poppy, and like this, it is very attractive to bees.

Cistus (Rock or Sun Rose) Nec./Pol. Shr.
Jun.–Jul., dry, salt tol., full sun.
To see just one Cistus in full flower on a sunny day, loaded with pollen-covered bees, is enough to captivate most people and start them off collecting a range of these beautiful free-flowering plants; but to see hillsides and sea cliffs covered with them, as is common in Spain and Portugal, southern France and the Mediterranean islands, is breathtaking.

The large central boss of stamens is invariably yellow and always contrasts well with the petals, be they white, rose-pink, purple or shades in between. Many species also have a distinctive 6–13mm (0.25–0.5in) blotch, usually dull red, at the base of each of the five petals. The satiny petals of the larger-flowered species are somewhat crinkled, like poppies, which presumably helps to strengthen and support them. The flowers will not open at all unless they receive direct sunlight, so choose a spot for your plants carefully; they also thrive best on dryish soils. The buds of many species colour well prior to opening, and are attractive in their own right; in some species they, and the leaves, are also sticky. Severe winters will kill off even large mature specimens, bur they are easily propagated by cuttings taken in August.

Cistus x corbariensis Rock Rose. All the rock roses are great pollen plants, thriving in sunny and dry conditions

C. x corbariensis ht: 1m *3ft* dist: 1–1.25m *3–4ft*. The dark sage-green leaves are up to 3.5cm (1.5in) long, and the pure white flowers are small in comparison with other species, but compensate for this by sheer volume of numbers. Hardier than most species, but certainly not completely hardy.

C. x cyprius ht: 2m *6ft* dist: 1.25m *4ft*. Clusters of 9cm (3in) pure-white flowers with crimson blotches.

C. x purpureus ht: 1.5m *5ft* dist: 1.25m *4ft*. The 10cm (4in) rose-crimson flowers have dark brown blotches at the petal bases. A very showy plant.

C. x 'Silver Pink'. Perhaps the most widely available hybrid, with 9cm (3in) silver-pink flowers.

Clematis Pol.
full sun.
Perhaps the most exotic and interesting of all the climbing plants, with something for everyone's taste, both with regard to flower size and colour. Not all are climbers; some interesting herbaceous types are also cultivated. No nectaries as such are present, although some species exude nectar from the mass of stamen stalks. The stamens in all species are yellow or pale lemon, and are a distinctive feature, contrasting well with the flower colour. The long anthers

C. armandii 'Apple Blossom', a somewhat tender evergreen climber which looks magnificent growing on walls or up trees

produce large quantities of pollen, and under suitably warm conditions the flowers may be worked by bees for both nectar and pollen.

The elegant divided leaves are always carried in opposite pairs, and in the climbing species have long stalks that twine vigorously round anything with which they come into contact. In deciduous species only the leaflets drop in the autumn, leaving the stalk to harden as it dries, to act as a long-term support – anyone who has tried to untangle Clematis branches when pruning will testify to the efficacy of these seemingly weak 'anchors'.

In spite of their reputation for requiring cool roots (conditions they naturally obtain by growing near the bases of trees), most will thrive as long as not in a 'hot spot' and able to get their roots into moist (but not wet or soggy) soil. Clematis also certainly have a preference for alkaline soils, and few if any Old Man's Beard (Clematis *vitalba*), which is native to most of Europe, will be seen in the wild where the pH is much below 6.5.

C. alpina ht: 2m *6ft* May. Lantern-shaped nodding blue flowers 5cm (2in) long, the petals of which are pointed. The outer stamens are infertile and strap-shaped. It is an ideal plant for trailing over a dwarf wall, or for clambering through shrubs. Makes a very pretty combination with the soft yellow and gently arching habit of Cytisus *x praecox*. Red, pink and white cultivars are also available. Pruning is not essential, but *alpina* can be vigorous on good soil, so may need shearing back.

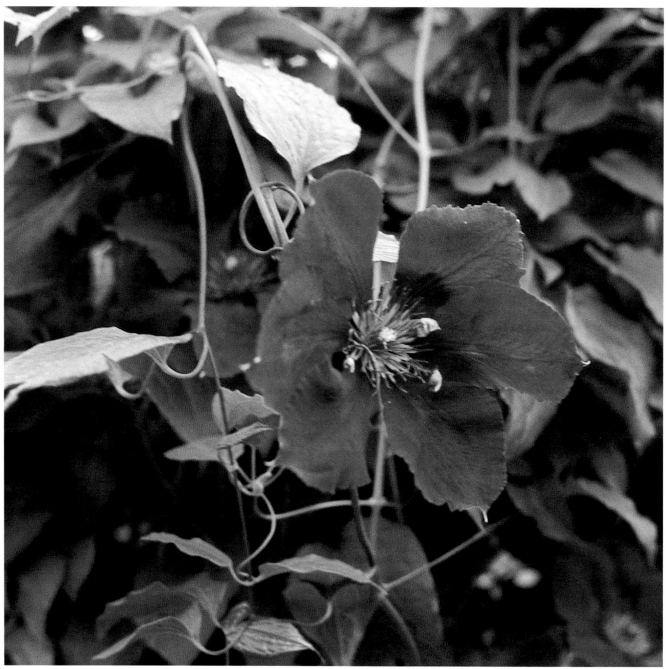

C. armandii 'Apple Blossom' ht: 3.5–4.5cm *12–15ft* Apr.–May. An irresistible evergreen with dark, leathery leaves, which set off the axillary clusters of white pink-shaded flowers perfectly. Definitely needs the shelter of a warm wall in northern districts, and even this may not be enough to prevent some frost damage. No pruning required.

C. heracleifolia H. ht: 1–1.25m *3–4ft* dist: 1m *3ft* Aug.–Sep. Fragrant flowers with pale blue, recurved petals. Needs staking.

C. integrifolia H. ht: 60cm *2ft* dist: 45cm *18in* Jun.–Aug. Blue lantern-shaped flowers 3.5cm (1.5in) across.

C. x jackmanii ht: 4.5m *15ft* Jul.–Oct. Stunning violet-blue flowers up to 14cm (5.5in) or so in diameter, produced singly or in threes. In February, cut back flowered shoots either to just above ground level or to within a couple of buds, or to where they were pruned to the previous season. This hybrid, together with the bulk of large flowered hybrids, does not produce any nectar.

C. montana ht: 9m *30ft* May. A vigorous and often rampant species ideal for covering large trees to a height of 6–9m (20–30ft) without difficulty, and so effectively that it is often difficult to identify the host! It will cover walls, sheds, old cars and other eyesores with equal ease, regardless of aspect. A superb plant, flowering freely year after year without any attention. *C. montana* itself is white, the pink-flowered form is 'Rubens', with bronzy leaves and shoots. Prune, if you need to, immediately after flowering; cut flowered shoots back to within a couple of buds of the main framework.

Left: Clematis *x jackmanii*

Opposite: *C. montana*

C. 'Nelly Moser'

The large flowered hybrids are the gardeners' favourite, because of their massive 13–23cm (5–9in) diameter flowers and their moderate vigour. Many cultivars are available, of which three are listed below.

'Mrs Cholmondely' ht: 3–4.5m *10–15ft* May–Sep. Large pale-blue flowers with pointed petals. Prune back to within a foot or so of ground level in February.

'Nelly Moser' ht: 3–4.5m *10–15ft* May–Jun. Pale-pink flowers with a wide carmine bar to each petal. Goes over very quickly if planted in hot, dry situations, but there may be a second flush of flowers in September. The most popular cultivar of all. Trim back flowered shoots after flowering.

x 'Ville de Lyon' ht: 3–4.5m *10–15ft* Jul.–Oct. Bright carmine-red flowers. Prune as for 'Mrs Cholmondely'.

C. tangutica ht: 4.5m *15ft* Aug.–Oct. Ideal for clambering over trees, shrubs and fences. Small yellow lantern-shaped flowers rather like *alpina*. Fluffy silvery seed heads through autumn and winter. No pruning is required.

A close-up of the *C.* 'Nelly Moser' flower

Colutea Nec./Pol. Shr.
Jun.–Sep., salt tol., full sun.
A Mediterranean shrub, it has become naturalised in some more northerly areas, and is common on rough ground around London and the Thames estuary in England, where beekeepers are finding it a good forage plant for both nectar and pollen. The Bladder Sennas, as they are known, are easily grown and have pea-like flowers and much-divided leaves.

C. arborescens ht: 3m *10ft* dist: 2m *6ft*. Individual flowers 2cm (0.75in) long, bright yellow-orange.

Coreopsis Nec./Pol.
Jun.–Sep., full sun.
Easily grown composites, which in their simplest forms are single-coloured with fine grassy foliage.

C. auriculata 'Superba' H. ht: 75cm *2.5ft* dist: 60cm *2ft*. Attractive ragged appearance to the petals, eye dull orange-red.

C. grandiflora 'Goldfink' H. ht: 23cm *9in* dist: 23–30cm *9–12in*. 'Flowers also ragged, but more evenly so, and clear yellow with a small orange-red eye.

C. verticillata H. ht: 60cm *2ft* dist: 45cm *18in*. Masses of 5cm (2in) clear-yellow flowers, with pointed petals.

In addition there are several annual cultivars available, the best known is perhaps 'Dwarf Dazzler', with its heavily zoned colouration, the eye is so large it almost swamps the ground colour. Not unlike Zinnia.

Cornus (Dogwoods) Nec./Pol.
A variable and decorative genus of plants. Some, such as the red and yellow stiff-stemmed dogwoods, are well known. Others, such as the elegantly tiered *kousa*, are rarely seen. The flowers of most species are as unremarkable as they are prolific, but in some the tight clusters of small four-or-five-petalled flowers, which provide easy bee access, are surrounded by large showy bracts.

See the below and opposite for ease of reference: those with coloured stems, and those with attractive 'flowers' (which are in fact bracts).

COLOURED STEMS ht: 1.5m *5ft* dist: 2–2.25m *6–7ft* May–Jun., full sun, semi-shade.

There is much more to this group than the stem colouration. The opposite pairs of leaves, which may be up to 12.5cm (5in) long, are handsome in their own right and usually colour up very well in autumn. Those cultivars which also have variegated foliage are particularly showy, providing year-round interest. Unfortunately, if the strong stem colouration is to be retained then the old stems should be cut down to within a few inches of the old wood in March, just before the new growth starts. This means no flowers for the bees. Compromise by cutting half the old stems down each year.

Although the coloured stems are most often pictured near water, the plants will in fact thrive equally well under dry conditions.

C. alba 'Elegantissima' Red stems, leaves broadly margined with white.

'Sibirica' Brilliant shiny red stems.

'Spaethii' A superb plant with red stems and strongly variegated golden foliage. Slightly less vigorous than the preceding cultivars.

C. stolonifera 'Flaviramea' With its yellow-green shoots, this is the perfect foil for the red-stemmed types.

FLOWERS

C. canadensis (Creeping Dogwood) H. ht: 15cm *6in* dist: 60cm *2ft* May–Jun., semi-shade. A dwarf suckering plant covered in summer with four-petalled white bracts atop crowded clusters of deeply veined leaves. Red tightly clustered fruits in autumn.

C. florida 'Rubra' Shr. ht: 2.75m *9ft* dist: 2.5–2.75m *9ft* May–Jun., full sun. The beautiful rose-pink notched bracts may be up to 10cm (4in) across, making this a very showy plant indeed. Couple this with good spring and autumn leaf colouration, and you have a good all-round garden plant. Several other cultivars are available. Prefers a neutral soil.

C. kousa chinensis Shr. ht: 2.75m *9ft* dist: 2.5–2.75m *8–9ft* May–Jun., full sun. Rather similar to *florida* 'Rubra', but with white bracts and red strawberry-like fruits. Not a plant that thrives for everyone, but once seen in its full glory you will be tempted to try it. Prefers a neutral soil.

C. mas (Cornelian Cherry) Shr. ht: 2.75m *9ft* dist: 2.5–2.75m *8–9ft* Feb.–Apr., full sun. If you had to choose just one Cornus it should be this one, for although it has neither the coloured bark nor large bracts of the other species, the clusters of tiny starry yellow flowers which crowd every bare twig in early spring lift the spirits, and are extremely attractive to bees if the weather is at all kind. The broadly ovate leaves are heavily veined. There is in addition a golden-leafed form 'Aurea', and an excellent variegated form 'Variegata'. If you are lucky you may also see the bright-red fruits which contrast nicely with the red-purple autumn leaf colouration. Easily grown on any soil, and completely hardy.

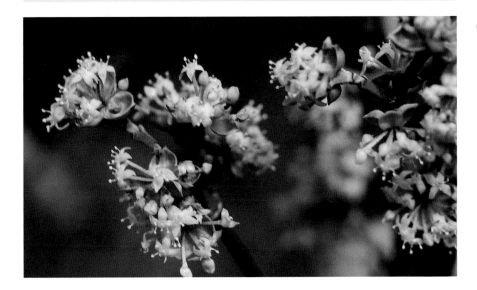

Cornus *mas* Cornelian Cherry

Corylus (Hazel, Cobnuts and Filberts) Pol. Shr.
Feb.–Mar., full sun, semi-shade.
The wild nut tree or shrub is too rampant for the average garden, but there are some dwarf cultivars that will yield useful crops of nuts, so long as you are not in an area ranged over by squirrels. It is not a particularly decorative plant, but does have good yellow autumn colour. There are also some highly decorative forms that make excellent garden plants.

In all cases, male and female flowers are borne separately on the same plants. The lemon-yellow pendulous male catkins, in groups of one–four, may be 5–7.5cm (2–3in) long and are a welcome sight on the hairy twigs in February and March, when they provide an easily accessible pollen source. The plant is wind pollinated and therefore as with most wind-pollinated plants, the pollen has a low nutritive value. However, it is so early in the year that it is a useful source of fresh protein to the bees when the weather is suitable for collection. In northern parts of Europe it is often too cold for the bees to forage on hazel catkins.

The female flowers appear as a cluster of red stigmas protruding only 3mm (0.12in) or so from the ends of plump buds, and you will need to look closely to see these miniature sea-anemone-like structures. The nuts are too well known to need description, but the bracts surrounding them are invariably removed before they reach the shops. This is a pity, since they are very showy – strongly veined with 'frilled' edges. The further north, the smaller the nuts become, so that in the Mediterranean they are enormous by comparison.

C. avellana 'Pearson's Prolific' ht: 2–2.25m *6–7ft*. The least vigorous and therefore most suitable cultivar. Produces round nuts.

'Aurea' ht: 1.25–1.5m *4–5ft* dist: 1.25–1.5m *4–5ft*. A yellow-green form that contrasts well with darker-foliaged plants. Rather slow growing.

'Contorta' ht: 2.5m *8ft* dist: 2.5m *8ft*. Commonly known as 'Harry Lauder's Walking Stick', this curiously twisted yet highly ornamental plant is covered in catkins in early spring. The foliage is also distorted. Slow growing.

C. maxima 'Purpurea' ht: 4.5m *15ft* dist: 3.5–4.5m *12–15ft*. The 'Purple-Leaved Filbert' has very strong leaf colouration, and even the catkins, bracts and nuts take on some of the purple colouration.

Cotinus Nec. Shr.
Jun.–Jul., full sun, shade.
Long-stalked, spoon-shaped leaves which are distinctly and pleasantly aromatic. Good red and/or gold autumn leaf colour (dependent on cultivar).

The four-petalled yellowish flowers, which are carried in loose pyramidal clusters, are tiny, less than 3mm (0.12in) in diameter. The whole infloresence

The catkins of Corylus

eventually lengthens and the long hairs on the flower stalks give a plume-like effect, earning the Cotinus its common name of Smoke Bush. Seed is rarely produced (unless warm weather prevails during the flowering period), most of the flowers falling off as soon as their colour fades.

C. coggygria ht: 3m *10ft* dist: 3–4.5m *10–15ft* Jun.–Jul. The plain-green form, all too rarely seen, is more showy, in a subtle way, than the purple forms, with its apple-green leaves and distinct seed heads which envelop the whole bush in a pink haze for many weeks in late summer and autumn. Golden autumn leaf colouration.

'Flame' ht: 3m *10ft* dist: 3–4.5m *10–15ft*. Particularly fine orange-red leaf colouration in autumn.

'Notcutts Variety' ht: 2m *6ft* dist: 2m *6ft*. Dark-red leaves, the flowers taking on some of this colouration.

With all species, once they have reached the desired spread, the annual growth can be cut hard back in January. As well as keeping the bush neat and preventing it spoiling other plants, this will encourage freer flowering and larger leaves.

✓   **Cotoneaster** Nec./Pol. Shr.
May–Jun., salt tol., full sun, shade.
Well over a hundred different choices of this invaluable nectar-producing plant are available. To the honey bee these plants are some of the most attractive grown in gardens. Small or large, they mass on them, and on the large tree species the buzz can often be heard from quite a distance. The average nursery or garden centre, however, may stock only six or eight, which may range from ankle height to 4–5m (15ft) plus.

The bulk of Cotoneasters are deciduous, but there are many which are evergreen. The flowers are mostly small, up to 1.3cm (0.5in) in diameter, and being white or pinkish are not usually regarded as showy. Gardeners, bees and birds alike will appreciate the colourful fruit (mostly red but sometimes yellow or black, depending on species or cultivar, about 6mm (0.25in) in diameter often plentifully produced in the autumn), and the brilliant red or copper autumn leaf colour of the deciduous kinds. These leaves may be retained, as with a beech hedge, until late winter in a sheltered spot.

Cotoneasters are susceptible to fireblight, a bacterial disease which can kill the entire plant, infection usually entering through the flowers. Many other rosaceous plants are also liable to attack. The disease decreases in prevalence from south to north in Europe, being most prevalent in southern France and Spain, although there have also been occurrences in northern Scotland.

C. conspicuus ht: 1.5m *5ft* dist: 1–1.25m *3–4ft*. An evergreen shrub with small, up to 6mm (0.25in), roundish, dark-green leaves. The plant is variable in height and habit. Some forms are low and spreading, while others may be 2–2.5m *6–8ft*, with arching branches. Try, if possible (if buying from a nursery that produces its own stock), to see the parent plant and ascertain if the plants being offered for sale have been propagated vegetatively or from seed. Vegetatively propagated plants will retain the characteristics of the parent plant, those from seed may well be very variable, particularly if other species or cultivars are grown in the vicinity and have been cross-pollinated by the bees. The flowers have conspicuous dark-red anthers. The fruit is shiny scarlet and is about 1cm (0.4in) across, and being relatively unattractive to birds is carried right through the winter.

C. dammeri ht: 23–30cm *9–12in* dist: 60cm *2ft*. A prostrate shrub ideal for covering banks in sun or shade, or as ground cover between other shrubs. Much more graceful of habit, with its slender creeping arched stems, than the stiff *horizontalis* types. The leaves are shiny, and on close inspection reveal an attractive net venation, reminiscent of many of the willows. Red fruits.

C. horizontalis ht: 45cm *18in* dist: 1–1.25m *3–4ft*. It is difficult to think of a more rewarding plant to grow: it seems to thrive on neglect and continues to flower profusely year after year, even on the poorest of soils, in sun or shade. Its normal horizontal growth habit can be reversed by planting it flat against a wall, so that its herring-bone shaped branches fan out over the wall instead of the soil; in this way it will happily reach 2m (6ft) or more with a minimum of support. It is a plant that the non-beekeeper may not want to go anywhere near on a sunny day, as the white flowers, pink on the outside, are invariably covered with every bee type.

Small, red fruits abundantly produced in the autumn hang on well into each new year (if the birds can be kept away), and then, in late autumn and winter, there is the added bonus of the small rounded leaves turning to red and then a burnished copper – delightful on even the dullest of winter days. The more petite variegated form 'Variegatus', with its white-edged leaves which suffuse with pink when the first frosts arrive, is also well worth growing.

C. horizonalis, a plant probably more attractive to bees than any other in the garden

C. x 'Hybridus Pendulus' ht: 1.5–2m *5–6ft* dist: 2–2.25m *6–7ft*. When grown on a 1.2–1.5m (5ft) stem (usually grafted on to *C. frigidus*), this must be one of the best small flowering and fruiting trees for a garden which welcomes bees. The branches arch downwards under the weight of the brilliant-red fruits, which contrast beautifully with the glossy leaves.

C. microphyllus ht: 1–1.25m *3–4ft* dist: 60–90cm *2–3ft*. Small-leaved evergreen with stiff main branches and younger stems of dull red. The scarlet berries complement the leaves perfectly, and some that have escaped the birds can be found even in late winter, partially hidden as they are by the stiff short side shoots.

Due to its limited stature it is frequently seen clothing walls below ground-floor windows. It is quite suitable for this if kept in order by pruning and regular tying in.

'Cochleatus' A prostrate, slower-growing form with paler and broader leaves, a superb plant for rock garden, alpine bed or dry wall. The dull-red stems and leaf stalks make a stunning winter attraction, especially when complemented by the conspicuous scarlet fruit.

Crataegus (Quickthorn, May, Hawthorn) Nec./Pol. T.
May–Jun., salt tol., full sun, semi-shade.
The number of common names that a plant has will often reflect its distribution. The greater the number, the wider the spread, and the genus Crataegus, which has many local names, is widely distributed throughout Europe, Asia and North America. A number of the species are known to produce ample pollen and nectar.

It is possibly one of the commonest and least fussy plants regarding soil and growing conditions; but for all that, whether it is for a hedge, specimen tree or shrub, if there is space then save a corner (just about anywhere will do) for a hawthorn. When flowering in late spring, there is a sheer mass of white or pink flower clusters that cover the entire tree, but double flowers are useless to the bees, and as many of the cultivars of this plant are double, bees ignore them. On warm days there is a heady sweet smell from the flowers, but the nectar flow is regarded as unreliable and unpredictable. Only about once in ten years or more does the flower produce a noticeable crop of honey, but when it does it is well worth waiting for as the honey has a delicious almond flavour. When nectar is present, it can be seen glistening as the numerous stamens open outwards in response to sunshine.

The flowers are followed in autumn by clusters of fruits, which in some species can be as large as crab apples, and just as showy. The leaves are lobed (sometimes almost to the mid-rib) or toothed and may colour well in autumn. Hawthorns are susceptible to the disease fireblight.

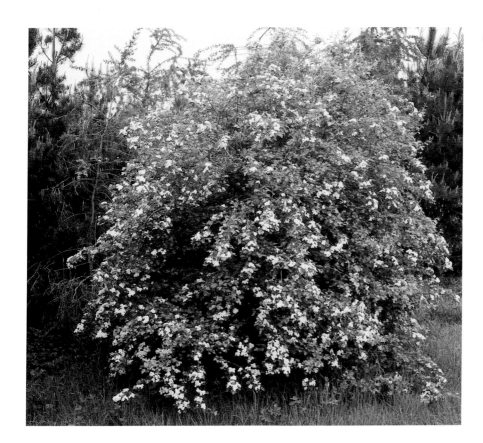

C. Quickthorn, May, Hawthorn

C. monogyna ht: 4.5m *15ft*. The most familiar of the European hawthorns, and far more common than *C. laevigata* (syn. *C. oxycantha*), from which it is not particularly distinct, except that it is thornier and more vigorous. The two species frequently hybridise in the wild. It has shining dark-red berries in autumn.

'Stricta' ht: 4.5m *15ft*. If space is limited and an upright tree is wanted, then this relatively small specimen should be suitable.

C. laevigata 'Punicea' ht: 3.5–4.5m *12–15ft*. Scarlet flowers.

'Rosea ht: 3.5–4.5m *12–15ft*. Pink flowers. Both this cultivar and 'Punicea' have small shiny dark-red berries in autumn.

C. x lavallei ht: 4.5–6m *15–20ft*. The 5cm (2in) stout spines of this hybrid are vicious, but there are many compensations. The ovate leaves are 7.5–10cm (3–4in) long, toothed in part, and dark glossy green above, turning the most gorgeous rusty red-brown in autumn. These will persist regardless of hard frosts right through to Christmas, contrasting well with the 2.5cm (1in) ovoid fruits, which are a wonderful orange-brown and very persistent. The flowers are white and large in comparison with the other species and cultivars described above.

 Crocus Nec./Pol. B./C.
ht: 15cm *6in* dist: 7–10cm *3–4in*
Feb.–Apr., full sun.
Although the Crocus (along with the snowdrop) is often thought of as the earliest harbinger of spring, there are in fact many late autumn and winter-flowering species and cultivars, all of which are rich sources of pollen at a time when few others are available. Those of most interest to the bees are the spring-flowering types. These provide the honey bee with a large early source of high-quality pollen as well as nectar. The bees are so eager to get at this wealth that they often force their way into the buds before the flowers are fully open – two or three bees, with large loads of bright-orange pollen on their legs, all together in one flower, is a not uncommon sight in warm weather. Forage sources of this quality are of inestimable value to the bee colony at this time of population expansion and recovery from winter problems.

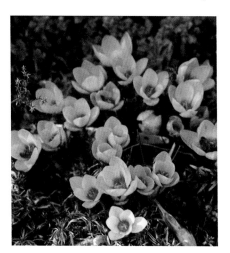

Crocus, easily grown and a large source of pollen and nectar

Additionally, there can be few more easily grown plants than the Crocus, with such a superb range of flower colours, produced when most other plants are at their least interesting. Colours include white, blue, purple and yellow, with intermediate colours, bicolours and bronzing of the outside petals of many varieties. How many of us could resist buying the corms if they were available when the plants were in flower? Small quantities can in fact be bought in this way as pot plants, but this is a very expensive way of going about it. Buy them by the hundred if you can – even for a small garden – in autumn, and plant them in a sunny position about 5cm (2in) deep, and a rich reward will be yours in less than six months!

The easiest way to plant into turf is to use a dibber (a broken fork handle sharpened is an ideal tool) or a bulb planter, and then just drop the corms in. Only the vigorous varieties (see below) are suitable for naturalising in turf or amongst other prostrate plants. I grow vigorous yellow and blue varieties through Polygonum *affine* (another excellent bee plant) and this gives the bees a second harvest from the same piece of ground, from June to September. You will probably want to keep any grass short in the immediate vicinity of bee hives, so do not be tempted to plant Crocus, or any other bulbs, here, since the foliage should not be cut back until it has died off naturally (or the bulbs will be weakened), and this may not be before the end of June, by which time the grass will be pretty long.

Grow the less vigorous varieties on rock gardens, scree beds, and on the edge of borders. Keep other vigorous plants from encroaching on them.

C. chrysanthus This species contains more cultivars than any other and is deservedly widely planted. Between two and five flowers are produced from each corm, and this spreads the flowering period from mid-January to late March. None of the cultivars is vigorous enough for naturalising.

'Blue Pearl' Pale silvery blue with orange stigma and a bronze base. Darker blue on the outside of the petals.

'Ladykiller' A striking colour combination: deep purple outside, edged with white, and white interior.

'Snow Bunting' Delicately scented, glistening white flowers with a golden throat and faint external purple feathering, orange stigma.

Seven or eight other *chrysanthus* cultivars are available in a range of colours from good bulb suppliers or garden centres.

C. tomasinianus Pale lavender-blue flowers in February, shaded silvery blue-grey on the outside. Strong grower, ideal for naturalising.

C. vernus Both this and its cultivars flower before the leaves are produced, and are two or three weeks later than the *chrysanthus* group. Often listed as 'large-flowered' or 'Dutch hybrids', the flowers are large and vulgar compared with, say, the delicacy of Crocus 'Snow Bunting'. Three to five flowers are produced per corm. They are, however, very showy and will compete strongly when naturalised in grass or low-growing plants. There is a wide colour range – blue, purple, white and yellow, with some cultivars, such as 'Pickwick', with stripes.

'Purpurea Grandiflora' A strong blue-purple 'Joan of Arc' White with orange stigma.

'Golden Yellow Mammoth' the name describes it perfectly. There can be few more warming sights on a sunny spring day than coming unexpectedly upon a mass of these rich-yellow flowers. The yellow cultivars are also popular with birds, which can destroy large numbers in their quest for nectar.

Cynoglossum (Hound's Tongue) Nec./Pol.
Full sun, semi-shade.
The common name refers to the shape and texture of the leaves, which may vary from lance-shaped to ovate, with a rough hairy surface. The small blue or purplish flowers are produced in profusion, and are very similar in size and shape to those of the forget-me-not; they also have the same white eye, fringed with hairs, and a short corolla tube leading to the nectary.

C. scoparius Common Broom

C. amabile 'Firmament' A(h). ht: 45cm *18in* dist: 23cm *9in* Jun.–Oct. The flowers are sky-blue, the foliage grey-green. Other named cultivars are also available.

C. nervosum H. ht: 60m *2ft* dist: 45cm *18in* Jul.–Aug. A superb plant with intense blue flowers on much-branched stems and long, narrow leaves.

C. officinale H. ht: 75cm *2.5ft* dist: 45cm *18in* Jun.–Aug. The wild Hound's Tongue is more interesting than pretty, its softly hairy grey leaves dominating the clusters of dull reddish-purple flowers. Certainly a plant that looks more at home in hedgerows and woodland than in a formal garden setting, but it does yield generous quantities of nectar.

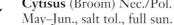 **Cytisus** (Broom) Nec./Pol. Shr.
May–Jun., salt tol., full sun.
A very easily grown genus of plants, with a host of free-flowering species and cultivars with flowers as plain or bold as could be wished for. The brooms, particularly the smaller-flowered species, are worked very heavily by the honey

The prolific Cytisus *x praecox*, a firm favourite with gardeners and bees

bee for nectar and pollen, the latter being gathered in profusion and carried as large brownish-orange loads.

Many of the general details on cultivation, flowering and pruning given under the Common Broom (*scoparius*) apply equally to the other species and cultivars.

C. scoparius (Common Broom) ht: 2–2.5m *6–7ft* dist: 1.5–2m *5–6ft* A plant familiar to those who know little or nothing of gardening, since it is common in the wild, particularly on dry sandy soils in association with heather, gorse and honeysuckle, throughout much of Europe.

   Every summer literally hundreds of gently arching, dark-green whippy shoots are produced; these rarely exceed 3mm (0.12in) in diameter, but they may be up to 60cm (2ft) in length. Every bud on these shoots will bear a golden yellow pea-like flower in the following late spring, turning the whole bush a gorgeous yellow from top to toe; and when a light breeze moves the flower-laden shoots and wafts the musky scent in your direction you will get an extra bonus.

The brown seed pods with their hard black seeds so freely borne are characteristic of all the brooms, and perhaps in this way they hope to compensate for the fact that they are not long-lived plants; eight to ten years is about as long as can be hoped for. Trimming back the flowered shoots immediately after flowering helps to keep the plants vigorous. Use shears for the pruning, and if you cannot cut through the shoots you are attacking reasonably easily, you are attempting to cut back too far. Brooms do have very small leaves, and are similar to evergreens because they change so little over the winter.

C. scoparius has spawned a host of showy cultivars, many of which are bicolours, such as 'Andreanus' (yellow and crimson), and these really should be seen in flower before you purchase these rather harsh colour combinations.

C. albus syn. *multiflorus* ht: 2.5m *8ft* dist: 2–2.5m *6–8ft*. The white Spanish Broom, free-flowering and a very good garden plant.

C. x beanii ht: 45cm *18in* dist: 45–60cm *18–24in*. This is a really superb dwarf shrub with rich golden flowers.

C. kewensis ht: 30cm *12in* dist: 60–90cm *2–3ft*. Cream flowers, and another really good plant.

C. praecox ht: 1.5m *5ft* dist: 1.5–2m *5–6ft*. A particularly graceful and floriferous shrub, flowers the same colour as *x kewensis*.

'All Gold' ht: 1.25m *4ft* dist: 1–1.25m *3–4ft*. Rather like a vigorous *x beanii*.

'Zeelandia' Mixed lilac, cream and pink colouration. Not all brooms flower in spring, and you might like to try *nigricans*, which grows to 1.2m (4ft) and has yellow flowers in late summer.

Daphne Nec./Pol. Shr.
Full sun.
Medium to small evergreen or deciduous shrubs, often with fragrant terminal or axillary clusters of flowers 1.3cm (0.5in) across. The four almost flat petals, which may be of unequal size, lead to a short tube in which lie the eight–ten stamens. The petals of the flower are actually the calyx, there being no true petals. The flowers are attractive to bees, providing (particularly in the case of *D. mezereum*) the weather is warm and fine. None of the Daphnes takes kindly to being moved, so be sure to buy container-grown plants.

D. x burkwoodii ht: 1m *3ft* dist: 60cm *2ft* May–Jun. Semi-evergreen with pale-pink fragrant flowers crowding the branches in early summer.

D. cneorum (Garland Flower) ht: 15cm *6in* dist: 60cm *2ft* Apr.–May. Wonderfully scented deep-pink flowers. This species is common in the mountains of Europe, where it sprawls over rocks quite happily with dwarf gorse and grass.

D. collina ht: 30cm *1ft* dist: 30cm *1ft* May. Dark-green leaves, fragrant rose-purple flowers. A rather slow grower.

D. mezereum ht: 1.25m *4ft* dist: 1m *3ft* Feb.–Mar. When it flowers well there are few more rewarding plants to grow. The bright-pink flowers, with their sequin-like surface and sweet fragrance, have to be the best thing to be found in the garden in February. A white form, 'Alba' is also very attractive. It does well on neutral soils, but will thrive even in limey ones. Birds, particularly finches, can decimate the flower buds of this and other species before they even open out, and they are also responsible for removing the berries before they give any semblance of a display.

D. retusa ht: 45cm *18in* dist: 30–45cm *12–18in* May–Jun. A rather stiff slow-growing shrub with white fragrant flowers, tinged with purple.

Deutzia Pol. Shr.
Jun.–Jul., full sun, semi-shade.
It is difficult to explain why these most elegant free-flowering shrubs are not more commonly seen in gardens, as their close relative, Philadelphus, has enjoyed much greater favour. The five-petalled, star-like flowers, 2.5cm (1in) in diameter, are really quite beautiful, usually pink on the outside and white within, and carried in loosely branched clusters. The ten stamens are like narrow petals and are forked towards the tip, with the yellow anther sitting in the fork. The three pistils are held well above the 'crown' of stamens.

D. x elegantissima 'Fasciculata' ht: 1.5m *5ft* dist: 1.5m *5ft* Jun. Fragrant bright rose-pink flowers.

D. x hybrida 'Perle Rose' ht: 2m *6ft* dist: 2m *6ft*. Pale-rose flowers.

D. x kalmiiflora ht: 1.25m *4ft* dist: 1.25m *4ft* Jun. Large pale-carmine flowers.

D. monbeigii ht: 1.5m *5ft* dist: 1.5m *5ft* Jun. Glistening white flowers, and small leaves that are white beneath.

D. x rosea ht: 1m *3ft* dist: 1m *3ft* Jun. There are several cultivars of this most graceful species, with white, rose or pink flowers. The cultivar 'Grandiflora', with its large white flowers suffused with pink, is particularly showy.

D. scabra

D. scabra ht: 3m *10ft* dist: 2.5m *8ft* Jun.–Jul. A rather upright species producing large clusters of erect, white, bell-shaped flowers often suffused with pink.

Dianthus
The pinks and carnations are wonderful garden plants, with their waxy, grey-green narrow leaves and brilliant single flowers, often most gloriously fragrant.

D. barbatus (Sweet William) Nec. Bien. Jun.–Jul., full sun. This is perhaps the best species to grow for honey bees. The domed flower heads, 10–12.5cm (4–5in) across, are made up of many individual flowers 2.5cm (1in) or so across, and can be obtained in a wide variety of colours from white through to dark red. Zonal flower markings in contrasting colours are an attractive feature of many of the plants, and the clove-like fragrance is a delight. Dwarf strains as low as 10cm (4in) are available. Seed should be sown in June for flowering the following summer. Do not expect a longer life span from your plants than two–three years.

✓ **Doronicum** (Leopard's Bane) Nec./Pol. H.
Mar.–May, full sun, semi-shade.
Large, bright-yellow flowers, as early as April, make Doronicum (in one of its forms), a must for the gardener and beekeeper alike. Although the daisy-like flowers are single, the petals are numerous and radiate from the domed centre, with its hundreds of individual florets. The long outer petals are well supported from beneath by two–three rows of sharply pointed bracts. Doronicum does well in any soil, and they are vigorous growers. The early-flowering species are most useful to the beekeeper.

D. caucasicum ht: 45cm *18in* dist: 30cm *12in*. Solitary yellow flowers 5cm (2in) across.

D. x 'Miss Mason' ht: 60cm *2ft* dist: 45cm *18in*. Pale yellow flowers 7.5cm (3in) across.

D. plantagineum 'Harper Crewe' ht: 1m *3ft* dist: 60cm *2ft*. Golden yellow flowers 7.5–10cm (3–4in) across.

There is one other plant I cannot resist mentioning, which although it is not a Doronicum is very similar, as indicated by the name Senecio *doronicum* (and also appreciated by the honey bee). I collected seed of this variable yellow-golden 'Doronicum' from the alpine meadows of the Maritime Alps, and have grown it for years in a shallow 12.5cm (5in) bed of soil lain directly on concrete, and it thrives! The flowering period is later: Jun.–Aug. All the Doronicums make excellent bee plants and cut flowers.

Leopard's Bane, makes a good show just as the daffodils are finishing. This is a particularly bee friendly plant

Echinops (Globe Thistle) Nec. H.
Jul.–Sep., full sun.
This is one of those plants that is so easy to grow that it never seems to get any special attention. In the long term this has earned it a reputation as a rather ordinary untidy plant, which, if it is given a little care, it most certainly is not. Handsome and distinctive is a more apposite description.

The spherical flowers, 5–7.5cm (2–3in) across, are packed with literally hundreds of small, star-like, narrowly lobed florets. The short floret tubes provide easy bee access, and sit atop a spiny cluster of bracts. These give the flower head a certain firmness, but they do not detract from its appearance as they are largely hidden by the floret petals. The bulk of the flower heads are carried at the end of long, erect stalks, and contrast well with the white woolly stems and thistle-like leaves, green above and grey beneath.

Even when the garden is full of flowers in July and August, Echinops are sought out by honey bees, and in spite of some reports that the nectar has a narcotic effect on them, this is not a side effect that I have personally ever noticed. Bumble-bees are, however, often heavily affected. They will often be seen, two or three at a time, sitting still on the flower head and if tapped on the back with a finger, appear to just hunch up a little, or put up a leg to ward you off.

It has been suggested that as they sup up a much greater volume of nectar than the honey bee, they pick up sufficient of the narcotising substance to immobilise them for a while.

E. humilis ht: 1.5m *5ft* dist: 1–1.25m *3–4ft*. Leaves less spiny than in many species, flowers steely blue.

'Taplow Blue' ht: 2m *6ft* dist: 1.25m *4ft*. Flowers pale blue.

E. ritro 'Veitch's Blue' ht: 1m *3ft* dist: 45–60m *18–24in*. Dark-blue flowers.

Echium Nec./Pol. A(h).
ht: 30cm *12in* dist: 23cm *9in*
Jun.–Oct., full sun.
These plants are very attractive to bees, providing both nectar and pollen in good quantity, but unfortunately are rarely in sufficient quantity to provide a surplus of honey.

E. vulgare (Viper's Bugloss) This plant is widespread in Europe and parts of Asia, and has been naturalised into North America. It thrives naturally on dry sandy soils and is an early coloniser of old gravel pits. The central stem and the narrow leaves are covered with stiff hairs, giving the whole plant a very rough feel. The stems are also speckled, hence the unusual common name.
   The 2.5cm (1in) flowers are carried in a line on lateral stems, which are at first coiled up but extend as the buds develop and bloom. The buds are pink, but gradually change to a bright blue funnel-shaped flower when fully open, with five protruding blue stamens carried on pink filaments. The pollen is blue as well. With a number of these uncoiling stems of bloom above each other, the whole effect is magnificent. The plant is really a biennial, but is usually treated as an annual in the garden.

E. lycopsis syn. *plantagineum* (Purple Viper's Bugloss) This plant is more restricted in its natural form, being local to the Mediterranean region, and the Channel Islands and Cornwall in Britain, although it does turn up in other areas as a garden escape. It was naturalised into Australia, where it became a major arable weed and earned the name of 'Patterson's Curse'. It was more popular among beekeepers.
   It is very similar to *E. vulgare* but is much softer to the touch, and the flowers, densely bunched on much longer side stems, start red in colour and turn purple-blue. Thanks to the efforts of the plant breeders the colour range has been widened to include white, pale blue and pink, and this has ensured its presence in many more gardens than previously. Sow seeds in situ during September or March–April, in drills 23cm (9in) apart.

'Blue Bedder' Deep-purple flowers.

'Dwarf Hybrids' Purple, blue, pink and white flowers.

Eranthis (Winter Aconite) Nec./Pol. B./C.
ht: 7.5–15cm *3–6in* dist: 7.5–10cm *3–4in*
Jan.–Feb., full sun, semi-shade.
An irresistible plant that associates well with snowdrops and spring-flowering cyclamen. The solitary 2.5cm (1in) cup-shaped flowers, with their six–eight rounded petals, are very similar in colour and texture to buttercups, and are a joy early in the New Year, especially for any bees that happen to be around, for the protected inner row of 'petals' is adapted into notched spoon-shaped nectaries, each glistening with nectar even on dull cold days. The branched anthers carry generous pollen loads, making this a very valuable bee plant. Beneath the flower is a much-divided leafy bract with twenty or so finger-like projections. These are a feature of all species and cultivars, but are more pronounced in some than others.

   Although they grow well enough in light soils, top dressing with leaf mould or peat will help to strengthen your 'colonies'. Plant about a hundred of them 5–7.5cm (2–3in) deep, and as early in autumn as you can buy them.

E. cilicicus Similar to *hyemalis* but less invasive, and the flowers are a deeper yellow.

E. hyemalis, Winter Aconite, one of the earliest bee flowers to bloom

E. hyemalis Probably the most popular species due to the ease of its cultivation. It will compete quite happily with Snowdrops and Crocuses.

E. x tubergineana 'Guinea Gold' Flowers large; perhaps the best of the bunch.

✓   **Erica** (Heaths) Nec./Pol. Shr.
Full sun, semi-shade.
The Ericas or heaths are closely related to the Callunas, and superficially bear them a close resemblance, but botanically they are quite distinct. There is a wide range of species with very different soil requirements (they do not all require acid soils) and growth habits, a small selection of which are described below. Honey bees work these plants avidly for both nectar and pollen. The honey produced from the Ericas is not classed as heather honey: this comes from the Callunas. Erica honey is a normal fluid, not a jelly, port wine in colour and very strong and bitter in taste.

Most of the individual species and cultivars will flower for around two months, depending on the weather, so although the flowering period shown against each species may cover several months, do not expect nectar and pollen from your one cultivar to cover this whole period. The individual flowers are usually carried in terminal clusters and vary in shape from bell to flask to cylinder. The calyx is far less prominent than that of ling, and is made up of four pointed sepals which are the same colour as the flower tube, spreading outwards as the flower opens.

If you wish to control the size of your plants then clip them over with shears immediately after flowering, with the exception of *E. australis*. I prefer to do this only one year in four or five, since the old flower spikes are very attractive. The *vagans* cultivars are outstanding in this respect. Armed with a knowledge of your own soil conditions and required flowering periods, take a trip to a good park or garden to see the mature plants before making any purchases, because although they may all sound rather similar they do look very different planted out.

E. australis ht: 1.25m *4ft* dist: 1–1.25m *3–4ft* Apr.–May, acid. The Spanish heath is a plant that is unfortunately not seen very often in cultivation in more northern areas, perhaps because it is not reliably hardy in all districts. However, I have seen these beautiful 1.25–2m (4–6ft) plants growing in cold parts of Britain, literally smothered with flowers, looking just like pink or white clouds year after year. Fragrant.

'Mr Robert' White flowers.

'Riverslea' Red-purple flowers.

Erica *x darleyensis*, a small spreading shrub with rosy-purple flowers. An Erica bed will give warm colour to the garden and flowers for the bees over a long period

E. cinerea (Bell Heather) ht: 30cm *12in* dist: 30cm *12in* Jun.–Oct., acid. The native bell heather is commonly found growing in association with Callunas on heathland and moors. Its short rounded flowers make for easy bee access and are carried along the whole length of the young shoots.

'Atrorubens' Long spikes of brilliant-red flowers.

'C.D. Eason' Very dark green foliage with pink flowers.

'Pink Ice' Again, dark-green foliage with vivid-pink flowers. This has to be one of the best heaths in cultivation.

E. x darleyensis ht: 45cm *18in* dist: 45cm *18in* Nov.–Apr. Slightly larger and more spreading than *E. herbacea*, with which it is often associated. The individual flowers are often longer too, and this enhances the effect of the protruding dark-brown anthers. Lime tolerant.

'George Rendall' Flowers deep glowing pink, carried over a long period.

'Silberschmelze' A really marvellous white-flowered hybrid with dark foliage and scented flowers.

E. herbacea syn. *carnea* (Winter Heath) ht: 30–45cm *12–18in* dist: 30–45cm *12–18in* Dec.–Apr. Its winter flowering, tolerance of alkaline soils and ease of cultivation have made this a very popular species with the whole gardening fraternity, and beds of them – often combined with dwarf conifers – appear everywhere. This is fortuitous, since the early spring-flowering forms are very popular with, and helpful to, honey bees.

'Atrorubra' Deep-pink flowers.

'Aurea' The foliage is golden in spring and summer, but bright coppery red over winter, and this acts as a perfect foil for the pale-pink flowers which are freely produced in February. Definitely one of the best of a very large number of cultivars.

'December Red' Dark foliage with showy magenta-pink flowers.

'Foxhollow Fairy' A most unusual cultivar with dark and vibrant magenta sepals. The flower tube is white at first but gradually takes on the same colour as the sepals. The protruding brown anthers give the final touch to a very attractive dark-green-foliaged plant.

'Springwood Pink' Trailing shoots with rose-pink flowers.

'Springwood White' A vigorous free-flowering cultivar producing numerous long trailing shoots packed with flowers.

'Vivellii' Very dark foliage turning bronze-red in winter. The flowers are a vivid carmine. A very showy plant. Rather more difficult to propagate than many other cultivars, so you may need to hunt for it and perhaps pay a little extra when you find it.

E. mediterranea syn. *erigena* ht: 1m *3ft* dist: 60cm *2ft* Mar.–May. This species has an erect growth habit, and the urn-shaped flowers are fragrant. Lime tolerant.

'Brightness' The bronze-red flower buds open to a rose-pink.

'Superba' ht: 2m *6ft* dist: 1.25m *4ft*. Pink flowers.

'W.T. Rackliffe' ht: 1m *3ft* dist: 60cm *2ft*. Similar habit to 'Brightness'. The white flowers have protruding brown anthers, and these look fine against the dark-green foliage.

E. tetralix ht: 30–45cm *12–18in* dist: 30cm *12in* Jun.–Oct., acid. The leaves of this species, native to Britain and western Europe, are arranged in fours, forming a cross, giving this plant its common name – 'the cross-leaved heath'. The leaves are small, dark green above, pale grey beneath, the margins of which are folded inwards and covered with short stiff hairs. The flowers, 6–8mm (0.25–0.33in) long, carried in terminal clusters, are urn-shaped and almost closed at the ends. At the 'mouth' the petals fold back slightly to form a small four-pointed collar. The shiny brown stigma extends beyond the collar, looking just like a too-long bell clapper.

'Alba Mollis' Small, distinctly grey leaves, white flowers.

'Alba Praecox' White flowers with grey foliage.

'Con Underwood' Crimson flowers with greyish-green foliage.

'L.E. Underwood' Silver-grey foliage with terracotta buds turning to pale pink.

E. vagans ht: 30–45cm *12–18in* dist:30cm *12in* Jul.–Oct., acid. The aptly named Cornish Heath may be found growing wild in abundance on the Lizard peninsula. The leaves are needle-like and are carried in whorls of four or five. The flowers are densely packed together, making this a very showy species. The small upward-pointing bell-shaped flowers are carried on fine long stalks, and the brown-tipped stamens add a distinct and pretty touch to the flowers, since they always exceed them in length. There is usually new growth of 2.5cm (1in) or so above the top of the flower spikes. Most cultivars will grow to about 45–60cm (18–24in), and although the colour range of *vagans* is narrow, it is not a plant I would want to be without. If you have the space and your soil is not alkaline, then you must grow at least two of the cultivars listed below.

'Fiddlestone' Rose-pink flowers.

'Lyonesse' Pure-white flowers, which remain an attractive brown throughout the winter period.

'Mrs D.F. Maxwell' Deep cerise pink.

'White Rocket' Fully 15cm (6in) flower spikes; fewer plants could be more aptly named. A magnificent plant.

Eryngium Nec. H.
Jul.–Sep., salt tol., full sun.
Striking foliage plants with spiny narrow leaves. The flowers of all species are surrounded by a ruff of toothed lance-shaped bracts, frequently the same colour

as the flowers. The individual flowers are tiny but are packed together in dense conical heads. The whole plant appears to have a most distinctive metallic finish. With all species, try to avoid root disturbance.

E. alpinum ht: 60cm *2ft* dist: 45cm *18in.* Large blue flowers.

E. emethystinum ht: 60cm *2ft* dist: 45cm *18in.* Smaller flowers than *alpinum*, but darker blue.

E. x oliveranum ht: 1m *3ft* dist: 60cm *2ft.* Green leaves and blue flowers, soft to the touch.

E. proteiflorum ht: 1m *3ft* dist: 60cm *2ft.* Flower head almost egg-shaped, 5cm (2in) long. The ruff of bracts are wider, longer and palish green against a darker green foliage.

Escallonia Nec./Pol. Shr.
Salt tol., full sun.
A handsome, easily grown and free-flowering shrub, available in a range of white, pink and red-flowered forms and in sizes to suit even the smallest garden. Under-rated as garden plants and, usefully, copious producers of nectar.

The small glossy leaves are finely toothed and, during a normal winter, will be retained. During severe winters, every leaf may be lost and new ones may not appear until summer, perhaps 60–90cm (2–3ft) back from the tips. The dead parts should be cut away, and by the end of the summer it should be difficult to see that any damage had occurred. To obtain the best display in colder districts some shelter from wind and frosts is very desirable.

The flowers have five rounded petals (with a short tubular base where the nectar collects), usually no more than 1.3cm (0.5in) wide. They are carried in terminal and axillary clusters. An outstanding plant for seaside areas in particular.

E. x rigida 'Donald Radiance' ht: 1.25m *4ft* dist: 1.25m *4ft* May–Oct. Showy, large rose-red flowers. Very hardy.

'Appleblossom' ht: 1.5m *5ft* dist: 1.5m *5ft* May–Oct. Aptly named, the pink buds opening to white. A very attractive plant.

'Edinensis' ht: 2.25m *7ft* dist: 2.25m *7ft* May–Oct. Graceful arching habit, flowers bright pink. Very hardy.

'Iveyi' ht: 2.5m *8ft* dist: 2.5m *8ft* Aug.–Oct. A vigorous plant with the largest leaves of those listed here, and large clusters of white flowers. Very hardy.

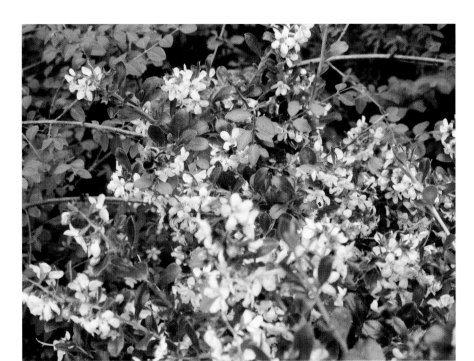

Escallonia Appleblossom

'Langleyensis' ht: 2.25m *7ft* dist: 2.25m *7ft* May–Oct. Arching habit, with deep rose-pink flowers. Very hardy.

E. rubra 'Woodside' ht: 45cm *18in* dist: 1m *3ft* Jul.–Oct. Rather spreading habit. The flowers are crimson and, though small, very freely carried.

Eschscholzia Nec./Pol. A(h).
Jun.–Oct., dry, salt tol., full sun, semi-shade.
Like most poppies, *Eschscholzia* is a real sun lover. The flowers remain closed in dull light but open increasingly to saucer stage, depending on the intensity of sunlight.

  The colour range is wide and vibrant, and the petals, often fluted in the newer hybrids, have the most wonderful satiny texture that, like the buttercup, reflects the sunlight. A lovely sight on a sunny day, with the extra delight of a few bees taking home loads of yellow pollen.

  The fern-like foliage is greeny-grey and is attractive in its own right, but it is also an excellent foil for the flowers. Sow in situ.

E. californica (Californian Poppy) ht: 30–45cm *12–18in* dist: 23cm *9in*. Yellow flowers. Many excellent hybrids have been raised from this species.

'Ballerina' Flowers mostly single, up to 6.5cm *2.5in* in diameter, with some semi-doubles, colours ranging through the reds, oranges, yellows to white. Rarely exceeds 30cm (12in) in height.

E. caespitosa ht: 15cm *6in* dist: 23cm *9in*. Altogether a more dainty plant in flower and foliage. The single flowers are lemon-yellow, up to 2.5cm (1in) in diameter, making it very suitable for edging or rock gardens. Sometimes sold under the name of Primrose or Miniature Primrose, and though these may be more attractive names than *caespitosa*, they are not valid.

Eucryphia Nec./Pol. Shr.
Full sun, semi-shade.
Another of those marvellous plants that, once seen in full flower, you just have to persist in trying to grow, even though it is not always reliably hardy, except in milder and coastal areas, or where very well sheltered from cold winds by a wall or other plants. In such locations it will, once well established, thrive and survive severe winters; there is one such superb flourishing specimen, well over 9m (30ft) high, in the gardens of a National Trust property in eastern Scotland, which is about ten miles inland, well north of the Forth estuary.

The waxy pure-white flowers, carried singly or in pairs, may be over 5cm (2in) in diameter, and are packed with masses of orange or yellow-tipped stamens, which produce abundant pollen over a very long period. The toothed, deep-green shiny leaves are rather leathery, usually with three–five leaflets.

All *Eucryphia* prefer lime-free soil, but can tolerate a degree of alkalinity as long as the organic content of the soil is high. Try to plant out your container-grown plants after all frosts have gone, and plant other expendable shrubs close to them to give some measure of protection during the winter. Cut these back to prevent over-crowding as necessary.

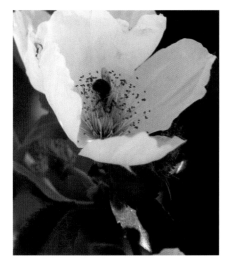

Eucryphia nymansayensis Nymansay

E. glutinosa ht: 3.5–4.5m *12–15ft* dist: 2.5–3m *8–10ft* Jul.–Aug., full sun. A towering column of white flowers during the summer, with the added bonus of good autumn leaf colour.

E. nymansensis 'Nymansay' ht: 6m *20ft* dist: 3.5–4.5m *12–15ft* Aug.–Sep. Fuller, overlapping petals. Very free flowering.

The bees work these Hypericum-like flowers for both nectar and pollen, and on warm days there can be one or two bees in every flower. This pollen is particularly valuable to bees, because they will be collecting their winter store of protein and will be feeding up to lay down body stores of fat and protein for the dearth period of winter.

Filipendula Pol. H.
wet, semi-shade.
The Meadowsweet (*F. ulmaria*), native throughout Europe, thrives in damp marshy places and produces rather feathery lop-sided spikes packed with small cream flowers, which attract bees in large numbers, many of which will be collecting delicate lime-green loads of pollen often mistaken by beekeepers as the pollen from lime trees. In spite of the sweet smell, nectar is not usually produced in quantity in Britain, although bees do work the plant for nectar in other areas of Europe. Unless you have a marshy area in your garden you would be unlikely to want to introduce the Meadowsweet to a garden setting. Heavy annual mulches can do much to make the other *Filipendulas* listed more suitable for non-marshy areas.

F. kamtshatica 'Elegantissima Rosea' ht: 1.25m *4ft* dist: 60–90cm *2–3ft* Jun.–Aug. Glistening satin-pink flowers.

F. multijuga syn. *palmata* ht: 1m *3ft* dist: 60cm *2ft* Jun.–Jul. Pink flowers.

F. vulgaris syn. *hexapetala* 'Grandiflora' (Dropwort) ht: 1m *3ft* 45–60cm *18–24in* Jun.–Jul. Creamy-white flower spikes and fine carrot-like foliage. Unlike other species this will also thrive in dry (normal) soils.

Forsythia (Golden Bell Flower) Nec./Pol. Shr.
Mar.–Apr., full sun, semi-shade.
There can be few shrubs that grow and flower so easily and profusely as the *Forsythia*, as evidenced by a trip through suburbia in spring – nearly every garden has at least one bush, which will invariably be covered from top to toe in a mass of flowers. Flowering early as they do, they brighten the scene when very few other plants are in flower, and they can provide a valuable early nectar and pollen source.

The nodding yellow flowers are shallowly bell-shaped, up to 3.5cm (1.5in) across, with four petals, and are carried in clusters, usually on short spurs before the leaves are produced. The young shoots and spurs are green-brown. The leaves can be up to 10cm (4in) in length, and vary in width; they may be shallowly or deeply toothed towards the tip. The plant's general habit is rather open, but with a tendency towards erect growth, particularly when cut back in order to contain them, as with hedges. This treatment has, in fact, the reverse effect from that desired, encouraging even more vigorous upright shoots with few flowers to be produced.

In some years flowering may be disappointing, particularly following a severe winter. This is usually the result of birds taking the plump flower buds for food; some black cotton draped over the bushes will help to prevent this.

Right: Fuchsia *magellanica* 'Gracilis Tricolour'
Far right: Fuchsia *microphylla*

F. x intermedia 'Beatrix Farrand' ht: 3.25m *11ft* dist: 2.5m *8ft*. Free-flowering and with the largest flowers, of deep canary yellow. The throat is a darker yellow-orange and the leaves are very deeply toothed.

'Spectabilis' ht: 2.75m *9ft* dist: 2m *6ft*. A superb free-flowering shrub slightly less vigorous than 'Beatrix Farrand'.

F. ovata ht: 1.5m *5ft* dist: 1.25m *4ft*. This species has deeper yellow, smaller, but much more broadly petalled flowers than the preceding cultivars, and is an ideal choice for the smaller garden.

Fuchsia Nec./Pol. H/Shr.
Salt tol., full sun, semi-shade.
The graceful pendulous Fuchsia flowers have a waxy beauty all their own. The upper part of the flower is tubular (long or short depending on variety), and from this narrow 'waist' the petals flare out to give a hooped-petticoat effect. Those types with double flowers – multiple petticoats, as it were – are of less interest, since although they do yield pollen, nectar access for the honey bee is rather restricted. This problem is even greater in varieties with long, narrow upper flower tubes, such a *F. thalia*. The outer 'petals' (actually sepals) are frequently in contrasting colours to the inner ones, from which they fold back. The crowning touch is the long protruding pistil surrounded by a mass of stamens which together almost double the length of the flower. An exquisite plant.

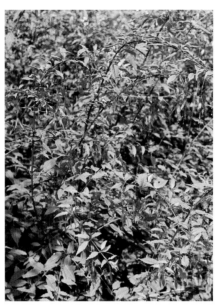

Far left: Fuchsias thrive in sunny spots and semi-shade
Left: Fuchsia *macrostemma*

The Fuchsias listed are hardy enough to become shrubs (with stems that persist through the winter) in the milder southwestern and coastal districts of Britain. They are, however, capable of regenerating from the rootstock in colder areas, provided some protection is given to the crown of the plant; this can be done either with a cloche or coarsely sieved peat.

F. magellanica 'Gracilis Tricolour' ht: 1m *3ft* dist: 1m *3ft*. Graceful arching branches, and dainty leaves margined with creamy-yellow, flushed pink and grey. Flowers small, with red sepals and purple petals. Slightly less hardy than the species.

'Mrs Popple' ht: 1m *3ft* dist: 60cm *2ft*. Large flowers with red sepals and purple petals.

'Riccartonii' ht: 1.25m *4ft* dist: 1m *3ft*. Graceful arching branches packed with small flowers with crimson sepals and purple petals.

All the more exotic 'pot-plant' Fuchsias will also grow well enough out of doors for the summer in cool temperate areas. Try bedding a few out in a sunny spot in June. Nectar production is obviously greater in sunny locations and districts, where the flowers may be worked with some enthusiasm by honey bees, but Fuchsias will also thrive in semi-shade. This semi-shade can take the form of a low wall or other plants, and this will help to minimise winter plant losses.

✓ *𝒢*

Gaillardia (Blanket Flower) Nec./Pol. H.
Jun.–Nov., full sun.
An unendearing common name for another member of the huge *Compositae* family of which the bees are so fond. *Gaillardia* stands out because it flowers for such a very long period, and will grow just about anywhere if it has full sun. The flowers are typically daisy-like, with several rows of ray florets. In most cultivars the florets are tipped with yellow or pale orange, the ground colour being red or red-brown. All are natives of central and southern USA, where in some areas they are important bee plants.

Perennial types can be propagated by division or root cuttings, and to retain their vigour they should be cut down quite low, and watered and fed before the first frosts. The annual types, of which several are available, can be raised from seed, which may be sown in situ in March/April.

G. aristata 'Croftway Yellow' ht: 60cm *2ft* dist: 45cm *18in.* Florets all yellow, centre yellow-orange.

'Dazzler' ht: 60cm *2ft* dist: 45cm *18in.* Orange tips, red centre.

'Goblin' ht: 23cm *9in* dist: 23cm *9in.* Yellow tips, red-brown centre. One of the most commonly seen herbaceous plants, which as well as all its other attributes makes an excellent cut flower.

G. pulchella ht: 40cm *15in* dist: 30cm *12in.* Mostly red-purple florets, otherwise similar to *aristata*, with which it has been hybridised to produce a range of variously coloured hybrids.

✓ **Galanthus** Nec./Pol.
ht: 15–18cm *6–8in* dist: 7.5–10cm *3–4in*
Jan.–Apr., semi-shade, shade.
How well both the English and French common names, 'Snowdrop' and *'Perce Neige'*, fit this hardy dwarf bulb. Cool shady growing conditions such as can be found beneath trees, where the soil may be bone dry in summer, suit the snowdrop very well. Given these conditions the clumps will expand at such a rate, even on a light sandy soil, that if they were not so welcome they might be thought invasive.

The flowering season is long – several weeks – and this would appear to be essential to ensure pollination in January, February and March. The buds are held erect at first, but later 'drop' as they break free of the enveloping sheath. The outer three petals, pure white, spread widely like a propeller, perhaps 3.5cm (1.5in) across, to reveal the short 1.3cm (0.5in) inner petals. These overlap and each is conspicuously but shallowly notched at the centre. Apple-green markings on both the inside and outside of the white inner petals vary with

Gaillardia '*Goblin*'

species and cultivar. The six anthers, like miniature spears, bear bright yellow/orange pollen. The scented forms smell of honey.

In suitable weather, bees will work snowdrops very heavily. It is an early source of valuable good-quality pollen, which will be seen as rather shiny yellow-brown loads on the legs of most of the foragers.

Snowdrops are one of the few bulbs that move best when green (that is, immediately after flowering). They are rarely offered for sale green, so try to beg a few clumps from a neighbour at the appropriate time. Plant them 10cm (4in) deep.

G. elwesii A variable species with relatively broad glaucous leaves. The inner petals each have two green spots which in some forms merge. The thick stems bear large egg-shaped flowers.

F. ikariae This species is easily distinguished by its shiny dark-green leaves. The inner petals are distinctly notched and have pale-green markings. Scented.

G. nivalis The common snowdrop, and naturalised in many areas. The flower stems are sturdy – rarely exceeding 20cm (8in), and the markings on the inner petals are dark green. Scented.

Leucojum, or spring snowflake, are similar to, but rather larger than, the snowdrop and more showy, and are preferred by some. They are not as widely grown as snowdrops, but do yield good early pollen and some nectar.

Gentiana (Gentian) Nec./Pol.
The very name Gentian evokes the clean freshness of the Alps, and the bright and variable blues of the flowers are stunning, although there are in fact other colours, including yellow and white.

Do not ignore them because your soil is not acid or is heavy: gentians are as variable in their soil requirements as they are in their growth habits and flower colouration – a species (or one of its many hybrids) can be found to suit most conditions. They do not like waterlogged soil or poor drainage.

Most species have a tufted carpeting growth habit, with opposite pairs of grass-like leaves arranged alternately. The blue chalice-shaped flowers, variously striped and/or spotted, flare outwards into five rounded or pointed petals. Although the stems may be rather lax, the flowers are held erect, and this ensures that the 6mm (0.25in) or so of nectar at the flower base is conserved for bees or other insects. The dwarf species are ideal for the rock garden, scree or terrace.

G. acaulis (Trumpet or Bell Gentian) H. ht: 15–23cm *6–9in* dist: 15–23cm *6–9in* Jun.–Jul., full sun, semi-shade. Deep-blue solitary flowers up to 5cm (2in) long and 2.5cm (1in) across, the throat spotted green and striped. Reputed to be rather fickle about producing flowers, but does well without any special attention.

G. asclepiadea (Willow Gentian) H. ht: 60cm *2ft* dist: 30cm *12in* Jul.–Sep., semi-shade. A most beautiful and floriferous species with deep-blue flowers with paler stripes carried on graceful leafy stems. Once established, do not disturb the clumps.

G. farreri H. ht: 15cm *6in* dist: 15cm *6in* Sep.–Oct. Showy 'Cambridge' blue flowers, spotted with greenish blue, terminal and solitary, on decumbent stems. Tolerant of some lime in the soil.

G. septemfida H. ht: 15–23cm *6–9in* dist: 15–23cm *6–9in* Aug.–Sep., full sun, semi-shade. Perhaps the easiest and most reliable species, thriving in almost any reasonable situation, where it will form large clumps with the usual trailing stems. Flowers up to 2.5cm (1in) or so long, carried in clusters of seven or so, purplish blue with markings on the inside of the petals disappearing into the paler throat. There are very finely branched secondary 'petals' between the larger petals, giving it the look of a gentianella rather than a gentian.

G. sino-ornata H. ht: 15–23cm *6–9in* dist: 15–23cm *6–9in* Aug.–Nov., acid, full sun, semi-shade. Large deep-blue flowers, 3.5cm (1.5in) long, with some green markings in the bold stripes on the corolla. Needs moisture without 'wetness', very free-flowering when conditions are right for it.

G. verna angulosa H. ht: 10–15cm *4–6in* dist: 15cm *6in* May–Jun., full sun, semi-shade. The grass-like foliage is often completely covered by the brightest blue flowers, 2cm (0.75in) in diameter, which have a white eye. The calyx is prominently winged in this variety.

✓

Geranium (Crane's Bill) Nec./Pol. H.
Geraniums are not the bright red-flowered bedding-plants, they are in fact *Pelargonium*, a completely different and less versatile genus, at least in northern European climates. The geraniums have everything to recommend them: ease of cultivation, long flowering seasons, lots of flowers, a wide range of colours, interesting leaves, not fussy over soil, and above all excellent bee plants. They are among the best of all herbaceous plants, thriving in north and south alike. The flowers, carried singly or in terminal clusters, are five-petalled, the lobes rounded and notched, either flat or shallowly bowl-shaped, and 2.5–5cm (1–2in) across. The ten stamens are long and conspicuous. The fruit or seed pod is distinctly beaked, hence the common name, and this splits when ripe into arched or coiled sections. The rounded leaves are palmately lobed, sometimes very deeply so.

G. cinereum H. ht: 15cm *6in* dist: 30cm *1ft* May–Sep., full sun. Deep pink, smallish bowl-shaped flowers with conspicuous dark-red venation and a dark eye. The leaves are grey-green. The cultivar 'Ballerina' is white with crimson venation and eye. Good rock garden plants.

G. endressii H. ht: 45cm *18in* dist: 45cm *18in* Jun.–Oct., semi-shade. Very pretty clusters of pale pink, red-veined smallish flowers set against grey-green leaves. There are several cultivars available, all of them with deeper pink flowers. A rhizomatous species, so take care when replanting or dividing.

G. himalayense syn. *grandiflorum* H. ht: 45cm *18in* dist: 45cm *18in* Jul.–Aug., full sun. Deeply cut leaves and flat, almost round, large blue-purple flowers with a white eye. Rhizomatous. If you like the colour but not the size of this

Geranium sanguineum 'Lancastriense'

species, the cultivar 'Alpinum' grows no higher than 23cm (9in). There is also a variegated form.

G. macrorrhizum H. ht: 23cm *9in* dist: 45cm *18in* Jun.–Jul., full sun, semi-shade. A real spreader, with small strongly aromatic leaves which may turn reddish in autumn. The small flowers are rosy-purple and are carried in clusters. Rhizomatous.

G. psilostemon ht: 90cm *3ft* dist: 60cm *2ft* Jun.–Jul., full sun. Vivid medium-sized crimson-magenta flowers with a black eye. The leaves may colour well in autumn.

G. renardii H. ht: 23cm *9in* dist: 23–30cm *9–12in* Jun.–Jul., full sun. Worth growing for the sage-green, softly hairy, lobed and scalloped leaves alone. The leaf surfaces are so heavily net-veined that the whole leaf is rather like a quilt. One form also has occasional splashes of gold in the leaves. The deeply notched, medium-sized, cup-shaped flowers are pale lilac, with darker venation. Short flowering season.

G. sanguineum 'Lancastriense' H. ht: 15cm *6in* dist: 30cm *12in* May–Nov., full sun. A wonderful little plant, almost too good to be true. The largish clear-pink flowers just go on and on, almost covering the small downward-flexed leaves, which are rather like a clasped bird's foot. My own plants seed themselves freely and thrive even in compacted gravel paths.

Geum Nec./Pol. H.
Showy herbaceous plants, superficially very similar to the herbaceous Potentillas. The leaves grow from the base, and are usually much divided.

G. rivale (Water Avens) ht: 30cm *12in* dist: 23cm *9in* May–Sep., wet, semi-shade, shade. There is a world of difference between this dainty native plant, with its small, nodding yellow-buff flower heads, and the much more showy open-flowered garden types. *G. rivale* has hairy, reddish-purple sepals almost as long as the petals, and the flower, which is usually bee pollinated, is so packed with stamens that nectar extraction is a frustrating business for the bees. The seed heads are beautiful, rather like pink hairy spiders. It grows well enough on most soils, but thrives under wet conditions on heavy soils, where little else that you want in your garden will grow. Not in the first rank of bee plants, but irresistible for anyone with wild garden aspirations!

G. x borisii ht: 30m *12in* dist: 23–30cm *9–12in* May–Aug., full sun. The orange-scarlet flowers contrast beautifully with the bright-green foliage.

G. chiloense ht: 60cm *2ft* dist: 45cm *18in* May–Sep., full sun. The bright orange flowers are carried in clusters on slender stems. Most of the *Geums* grown in gardens are cultivars of *chiloense*, namely 'Mrs Bradshaw' (bright scarlet), 'Lady Stratheden' (golden yellow). Both these cultivars are, however, semi-double and therefore rather difficult for bees to work. The 1.3cm (0.5in) diameter flowers of both *x borisii* and all the *chiloense* cultivars have rather crinkly petals.

Hamamelis (Witch Hazel) Pol. Shr.
ht: 3m *10ft* dist: 2.5–3m *8–10ft*
Dec.–Mar., acid, full sun, semi-shade.
The fragrant yellow flowers of the rather gaunt Asian and eastern North American witch hazels are exotic. The four or more crinkly and strap-shaped

Hebe 'Blue Gem'. The shrubby Veronicas are very attractive to bees

petals push through the clusters of plump pale-brown flower buds on the leaf-less branches in very early spring. Each of the 6mm (0.25in) chalice-like calyces has four short full-red pointed sepals which give an attractive and contrasting dark eye to the flowers. The very open nature of the flowers ensures that the pollen is freely available, once these curious sheath-like sepals have released the anthers. The leaves are very similar to the hazel (see Corylus), but are more heavily veined and usually turn butter-gold in autumn.

Not very fast-growing plants, but they will eventually become too large for most gardens, although this rarely seems to stop the enthusiasts from cramming them in, and you can cut back any excessive growth from December to March and use it for flower arrangements, for which it is superb.

Plant groups of snowdrops and blue and yellow Crocus beneath the shrub to provide a cheerful sight for both gardener and bee in the late winter.

H. x intermedia 'Jelena' Dense clusters of large – well over 2.5cm (1in) – coppery-red flowers. Quite stunning. Red-orange and scarlet autumn leaf colouration.

H. mollis 'Pallida' Pale yellow flowers very freely carried. Autumn leaf colour yellow. Usually quite freely available and deservedly so, for this is a first-class plant.

 Hebe Nec. Shr.
Salt tol., full sun.
It is hardly surprising that the Hebes were for many years grouped botanically with the Veronicas, of which they are the shrubby counterparts. Not all species, however, have the very long flower spikes of the Veronicas, but those that do, such as the *speciosa* hybrids, are amongst the most handsome of easily grown evergreen shrubs; unfortunately they also appear to be the least hardy. To make certain you are buying species likely to survive in your area, visit a local botanic garden or large park and take note of which species are grown there.

Given reasonable conditions, Hebes grow quickly and flower profusely. The small tubular flowers have four petals, one 'above' and three clustered below. There is no difficulty with nectar extraction, and some cultivars, such as 'Carl Teschner', will be alive with bees on a sunny day.

The leaves, which may be narrow and up to 10cm (4in) long, or, at the other extreme, compressed and scale-like, are carried in opposite pairs. If you must grow species which are not reliably hardy, then try and choose a sheltered spot. All the plants listed below are reasonably hardy and will survive in most cool temperate climates, such as the British Isles.

H. x andersonii 'Midsummer Beauty' ht: 1.25–1.5m *4–5ft* dist: 1.25–1.5m *4–5ft* Jun.–Oct. A marvellous long-flowering cultivar with lavender-blue flowers and long narrow leaves.

Hedera *helix* Common Ivy

H. armstrongii ht: 1m *3ft* dist: 1m *3ft* Jul.–Aug. Cupressus-like shoots of olive green, yellow at the tips, with clusters of tiny white flowers. Rather stiff in habit.

H. x 'Autumn Glory' ht: 90cm *3ft* dist: 60cm *2ft* Aug.–Nov. The blue-violet flowers are carried in short clusters above the dark oval leaves.

H. brachysiphon ht: 1.25m *4ft* dist: 1m *3ft* May–Jun. Dense clusters of pink-tipped buds, opening to white, crowd the branches in spring, beautifully complementing the small grey stalkless leaves. The cultivar 'White Gem' is rather less vigorous.

H. x 'Carl Teschner' ht: 23cm *9in* dist: 60cm *2ft* Jun.–Aug. Short clusters of lavender-blue flowers with a white throat. The wiry stems are a dull burgundy-red and the leaves small and narrowly elliptic. A fine ground-cover plant.

H. x 'Great Orme' ht: 1m *3ft* dist: 1m *3ft* Aug.–Oct. Leaves lance-shaped, up to 7.5cm (3in) long. The flowers are bright pink in long tapering clusters. A most elegant plant and hardier than most of the other *speciosa* hybrids – well worth trying.

'Marjorie' ht: 1m *3ft* dist: 1m *3ft* Jul.–Sep. A very hardy cultivar with blue-mauve flowers that fade to white, carried in clusters 7.5cm (3in) long.

Hedera 'Dentata Variegata'

H. pinguifolia 'Pagei' ht: 23cm *9in* dist: 45cm *18in* May–Jun. Due in part to its undoubted hardiness, this is probably the most commonly seen cultivar in cultivation. The elliptic grey leaves are often margined dull red, especially in winter. In May the short clusters of white flowers with their distinct reddish-brown anthers cover the whole plant, and are a splendid sight. Grow it close to blue winter-flowering pansies, purple Aubrieta and blue Lithodora, with a few winter aconites scattered around.

Hedera (Ivy) Nec./Pol. Shr.
ht: 1–1.25m *3–4ft* dist: 60–90cm *2–3ft*
Sep.–Dec., full sun, semi-shade.
The common ivy, Hedera *helix*, is a familiar sight as it climbs up and sometimes over buildings and trees in town and country alike. The climbing shoots (which will trail equally well if there is nothing for them to cling to) are in fact the juvenile growth phase, and will bear 'typical' leathery ivy leaves with five pointed lobes, the two basal ones with a deep cordate base. Ivy is not a parasite and does not harm trees it climbs up. It is not necessary, therefore to follow the practice of killing ivy to protect the tree, particularly as a large ivy provides a lot of food and shelter for birds as well as forage for bees.

As the plant ages, and typically when it reaches the top of a building or tree, the whole growth pattern changes. Much thicker shoots without any tendency to climb are produced, and it is these shoots, and only these, that produce flowers and fruit once they reach sunlight. The leaves on these shoots have little or no lobing and are broadly oval in shape. This second growth phase is known as arborescent (or adult).

The juvenile phase is of no interest to us at all as a bee plant. The arborescent phase may not, however, be reached for fifteen–twenty years, and not many of us are prepared to be this patient! Interestingly, cuttings taken from arborescent shoots will, once rooted (and this can be a very slow process indeed), retain this characteristic, allowing the gardener to have 30–60cm (1–2ft) ivy bushes without any trailing shoots. Only a few ivy fanatics would bother to go to this much trouble, but there are one or two very nice named cultivars that might be worth a try if you are looking for a very late source of a really concentrated nectar.

Flowering in late September and October, ivy provides the last nectar and pollen forage for the honey bee. Numerous large pinkish-brown loads of pollen are collected at the same time as nectar. In some parts of Britain beekeepers rely on ivy to provide most of their colonies' winter stores. The honey is high in sugar glucose, and therefore crystallises very quickly, but usually this does not cause any problems. Some idea of the concentration of the nectar can be gauged by the attraction it has for all types of flies, wasps and other insects, as well as bees. Ivy is, however, such a common plant, in all parts of Britain at least, that it really is not worth planting.

The individual flowers are around 6mm (0.25in) in diameter, five-pointed and greenish, with a yellow central disc from which nectar is secreted. Each flower is on a long stalk, and there may be thirty or more flowers in each head. The flower stem may bear many secondary flower heads. The fruits are black, up to 8mm (0.33in) in diameter.

Remember that you are very unlikely to be able to buy arborescent forms of any of the species or cultivars listed below, but they are all good garden plants in their own right, and your patience will eventually be rewarded when they finally – after perhaps fifteen years – start to produce arborescent flowering shoots.

H. colchica Very large leaves and freer-flowering than the variegated type.

'Dentata Variegata' A really nice cultivar with variable yellow variegation around the outside of the leaves. It is absolutely hardy.

H. canariensis 'Gloire de Marengo' syn. 'Ghost Tree', 'Variegata', *algeriensis* 'Gloire de Marengo'. Large handsome grey-green leaves with variable creamy variegation around the outside of the leaves. Die-back of shoots may be a problem in severe winters.

Helianthemum Rock Rose

Helianthemum (Rock Rose) Nec./Pol. Shr.
ht: 23cm *9in* dist: 23–30cm *9–12in*
May–Jul., dry, salt tol., full sun.
Descriptions and recommendations for Halimum and *x* Halimocistus, which are very similar to Helianthemum, are also given below.

As the name implies, these dwarf plants positively thrive in full sun and, indeed, without it the masses of brilliant five-petalled flowers, in size and form rather like those of Potentilla, stay slightly closed on the ends of the thin wiry stems. The grey-green leaves contrast well with the brightly coloured flowers. Nectar is not produced in any great quantity unless the weather is very hot, but the large amounts of pollen carried over a very long season help to compensate for this.

None of the rock roses is particularly hardy, but they will withstand quite severe frosts if the soil is dry, so they do very well on hot dry banks, in or on walls and on light sandy soils. I have several plants in a really dry soil growing through gravel on a driveway, and they obviously enjoy this situation, for they never stop flowering from May to July. Cuttings root easily if taken in August.

Several seed firms now offer seed, usually of mixed colours of yellow, orange, pink and scarlet; sow in April to flower the following year (*x* Halimocistus is a hybrid and cannot be raised from seed, so cuttings have to be taken).

Helianthemum *nummularium*

H. nummularium 'Ben Nevis' Deep yellow with a deeper eye. Foliage green.

'Fire Dragon' Orange-red flowers.

'The Bride' Creamy-white flowers with a yellow eye.

'Wisley Pink' Clear-pink flowers with a shaded orange eye.

There are many other cultivars and an increasing number of seed-raised plants; take care when selecting plants, especially on a dull day when the flowers are not open, that you do not buy any with double flowers.

Halimum ht: 90cm *3ft* dist: 60–90cm *2–3ft.* Rather larger in all its parts than Helianthemum but similar in other respects. All the species have yellow or white flowers.

x Halimocistus (Halimum x Cistus) ht: 60cm *2ft* dist: 60cm *2ft* Blends the characteristics of both genera (see Cistus*)* and has slightly wider leaves. The species *wintonensis* is attractive, with its large white satin-like flowers, with dark crimson-maroon markings 'feathering' down to the yellow-stained petal bases.

Helleborus (Hellebore or Bear's Foot) Nec./Pol. H.
Full sun, semi-shade.
Most valuable evergreen perennials flowering in late winter and early spring,

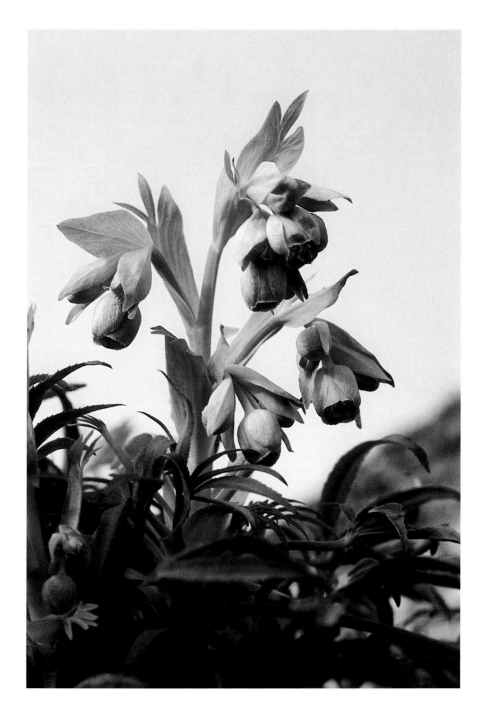

Helleborus *lividus corsicus* syn. *corsicus*

Helleborus *orientalis.* Colours range from white, to pink, to dark purple

producing copious amounts of both nectar and pollen. The handsome toothed, leathery leaves are divided into between three and twelve leaflets. The flowers may be carried singly or in nodding clusters, and vary in shape from flat to cup-shaped. The five or six 'petals' (actually sepals) are blunt and overlap each other, the true petals are adapted into boomerang-shaped nectaries 8mm (0.33in) long, surrounding the mass of anthers. The flower structure is very similar to that of the winter aconites. Always buy container-grown plants, since hellebores do not like root disturbance.

H. atrorubens ht: 30cm *12in* dist: 30cm *12in* Feb.–Mar. Deep red-purple 5cm (2in) flowers, greenish within, carried in clusters. Clump-forming.

H. lividus corsicus syn. *corsicus* (Corsican Hellebore) ht: 60cm *2ft* dist: 60cm *2ft* Feb.–Apr. The glossy three-lobed leaves are sharply toothed, and these gradually deteriorate as new ones are produced from the centre of the rootstock after flowering. It is best to cut back the old shoots in June after flowering, unless you wish to leave one or two to produce seed, which they will do very readily. The cup-shaped flowers are pale apple-green and are present in bud form from

Helleborus *orientalis*, the Lenten rose

January. A really tough hardy plant which, along with many of the other helle-bores, has what landscape designers like to term 'architectural qualities'.

H. foetidus ht: 60cm *2ft* dist: 60cm *2ft* Feb.–Apr. Surely this must be one of Europe's finest native plants, with its much-divided, narrow, dark-green leaves, for it always looks good but never more so than when the clusters of pendulous pale-green flowers with purple edge striations are produced. The bracts that subtend the flowers can also be very showy, with finger-like projections that make them look like small palm trees. Do not be put off growing this wonder-ful plant by its common name – Stinking Hellebore.

H. niger (Christmas Rose) ht: 30cm *1ft* dist: 30cm *1ft* Dec.–April. The flower-ing period of this species is very variable, in spite of its common name. The flowers are usually white, but may be tinged with pink or green. With flowers kept under cloches, to preserve their whiteness, I have seen honey bees work-ing them on Christmas Day in South West England. The cultivar 'Potter's Wheel' has very large, 10–2.5cm *4–5in*, pure-white flowers, and is a sight to behold when in full flower, pushing up through the winter snow.

H. orientalis (Lenten Rose) ht: 60cm *2ft* dist: 60cm *2ft* Feb.–Mar. The 7.5cm (3in) bowl-shaped flowers are rather similar to those of *niger*, but they come in a range of colours from white to pink through to dark purple, and some have glorious spotting in contrasting colours.

Hydrangea Nec./Pol. Shr.
semi-shade.
The Hydrangeas are excellent and easily grown garden plants, producing large rounded flower heads towards late summer. Unfortunately, many of the most commonly grown *macrophylla* (syn. *hortensis*) cultivars produce a preponderance of the more showy but sterile, or semi-sterile, individual flowers, which are virtually useless for honey bees. The ratio of fertile to sterile flowers can vary considerably with cultivar, so it is vital to do some research before making your choice. Any of the species listed below, or cultivars from the so-called Lacecap groups, can be bought unseen in the knowledge that they produce large numbers of fertile flowers.

The sterile four-sepalled 'flowers' are too well known to require a detailed description. Each tiny 6mm (0.25in) flower is star-like, the individual petals forming boat-shaped nectar carriers, and the mass of individual flowers, with their pale lemon or blue-tipped anthers, in strong light are not unlike a bright massed galaxy. The leaves are generally large and handsome, frequently taking on bronze tints before they fall.

Contrary to popular opinion Hydrangeas do not need acid soils to do well, but if grown on shallow chalky soils the leaves will show pale-yellow patches, and blue-flowered cultivars will turn pink. This can be counteracted by mulching with peat and regular treatment with bluing compounds, which are readily available from garden centres.

H. anomala petiolaris Jun.–Jul. A vigorous and attractive climber with broad pale-green leaves which turn butter-yellow in autumn. Even young plants produce aerial roots on the pale-brown stems, which quickly anchor themselves to just about any surface. Easily enough controlled by regular pruning which, since it is capable of reaching 10m *30ft* or more, will usually be necessary. If you neglect your pruning, then be prepared to have to take a saw to the limbs, which can easily reach arm thickness! The flower heads are greenish white and up to 25cm (10in) across, with a fringe of sterile flowers.

H. paniculata 'Grandiflora' ht: 2m *6ft* dist: 1.5m *5ft* Aug.–Oct. Dense lilac-like (both in size and shape) heads of creamy white flowers – fertile and infertile mixed together – which age to pink. The old flower heads should be cut well back after flowering, and they can be dried and used for winter decoration if required. If left until spring their frost-laden tracery can be enjoyed through the winter. Certainly one of the best of all autumn-flowering shrubs.

H. quercifolia ht: 1.5m *5ft* dist: 1.25m *4ft* Aug.–Sep. As the name suggests, the leaves strongly resemble those of the oak. White flowers similar to the Lacecap types listed in the below. Excellent autumn leaf colouration.

H. villosa ht: 2m *6ft* dist: 1.5–2m *5–6ft* Aug.–Oct. Leaves and stems densely hairy. Beautiful large lilac-blue sepals, which are also toothed. Perhaps needs more shade than other species, and this in turn gives some protection to the easily frost-damaged new growth in spring.

LACECAPS Jul.–Sep.

Rather flat heads of fertile flowers, fringed with sterile ones. All are excellent garden plants.

'Blue Wave' ht: 2m *6ft* dist: 1.5–2m *5–6ft*. Outer sepals may vary from pink to blue, depending on soil type.

'Lanarth White' ht: 1.25m *4ft* dist: 1.25m *4ft*. Outer sepals white, inner ones blue or pink.

'Tricolor' ht: 2m *6ft* dist: 1.5–2m *5–6ft*. Leaves variegated with grey and pale yellow. Flowers white to pale pink.

Hypericum Pol. Shr.   ✓
The shrubby golden-flowered St John's Worts are adaptable and easy plants to grow, as witnessed by the large number of species and cultivars that have naturalised themselves in Britain and other areas of Europe. In spite of this tendency in some to 'take over', they are a good choice for the shrub border or rock garden.

   Depending on their size, the flowers, which may be carried over many months, can be up to 7.5cm (3in) across, and are packed with literally hundreds of the most delicate thin stamens, topped with bifid anthers positively dripping with pollen. As the five rounded petals open, the anthers themselves fold back to reveal the stigmas arising from the typical onion-shaped base. Once flowering is finished this swollen base becomes an attractive fruit in some species, and the calyx may take on red-orange colouration. Some species also have good autumn leaf colour.

H. androsaemum ht: 60–90cm *2–3ft* dist: 45–60cm *18–24in* Jul.–Sep., semi-shade, shade. The small pale-yellow flowers are carried in terminal clusters of up to five flowers. When the petals fall the calyx becomes red-green, and in the autumn the large palish-green leaves also take on the same colours, making a very pretty picture, especially when the red berry-like fruits, later turning to purple-black, have also formed.

H. calycinum Rose of Sharon

H. calycinum (Rose of Sharon) ht: 45cm *18in* dist: 45cm *18in* Jul.–Sep., semi-shade, shade. Definitely an invasive species, with a strongly suckering habit. No empty neighbouring piece of ground or even path is safe from its wanderings. It can be forgiven anything in return for its pale-gold flowers (carried singly) which are a full 7.3cm (3in) across.

The rounded petals are widely spaced and the centre is packed with hundreds of yellow stamens, each topped with a dull-red anther. The leaves are large, and are dark green and rounded – a nice complement to the flowers. The plants can become very untidy if left unpruned.

H. x indorum 'Elstead' ht: 1–1.25m *3–4ft* dist: 60–75cm *2–2.5ft* Jul.–Sep., semi-shade, shade. The flowers are small and yellow, but they are followed by the most exquisite coral-pink fruits in autumn.

H. olympicum ht: 15–23cm *6–9in* dist: 23–30cm *9–12in* Jun.–Aug., full sun. Forms a dense mound covered with large golden 5cm (2in) flowers and small blue-green leaves. Ideal for wall crevices or rock gardens. *H. olympicum citrinum* is a showy lemon-yellow form.

H. patulum 'Hidcote' ht: 1.25–2m *4–6ft* dist: 1m *3ft* Jul.–Oct., full sun, semi-shade. 'Golden Saucer' is a good name for the clusters of large satin-textured flowers with orange anthers, which are freely carried throughout the summer. The leaves are dark green above, pale beneath and semi-evergreen. Quite simply 'a winner'.

Iberis Nec./Pol.
Dry, full sun.
The candytufts are very free-flowering and extremely easy to grow, even on the poorest and driest of soils. The flat flower heads, which are up to 5cm (2in) in diameter, contain many florets, the inner ones small, the outer progressively larger. Each floret has four petals, the outer two of which are considerably larger than the inner, thus providing an excellent work platform for the bees.

I. saxatilis H./Shr. ht: 15cm *6in* dist: 30cm *12in* May–Jun. The dark-green prostrate mats of foliage are smothered with dazzling white 15cm (6in) flower spikes in spring. An excellent rock garden plant. Cut back the flower spikes as soon as flowering is finished.

I. sempervirens 'Snowflake' H./Shr. ht: 30cm *12in* dist: 23cm *9in* Jun. As the pure-white rounded flower heads are 5cm (2in) in height it is a shade tall for the rock garden.

I. umbellata 'Dwarf Fairy' A(h). ht: 30–40cm *12–15in* dist: 23cm *9in* May–Oct. Easily raised from seed sown in situ, giving a variety of really pretty 'candy' coloured flowers – magenta, pinks, lavender and white – over a very long season. Left to their own devices the flattened seed cases will sow next year's crop for you, but they may not grow exactly where you want them to.

Ilex (Holly) T./Shr.
May–Jun., salt tol., full sun, semi-shade.
The hollies are native to most of Europe, North and South America and Asia, where they are common large shrubs or trees in the wild. Holly is known to most people; if not in the wild, then through Christmas wreaths, decorations and cards. It is part of the traditional Christmas scene.

The thick leathery leaves are like burnished leather, with stiff prominent prickles pointing in all directions from the leaf margins. The branches retain their green colouration for many years, and in variegated forms pink or dark red striations are an additional attraction.

The fragrant flowers are small and white and are carried in the leaf axils. They secrete nectar freely and are well worked by honey bees. Male and female flowers are carried on separate plants, and this explains why many hollies never have berries (as these are obviously males or, to confuse the issue further, females without the benefit of local males!). An inspection of the flowers will, however, reveal the true state of things. The females bear berries, but will have no pollen. If you want berries then you will have to plant male and female plants in your garden, unless there are male plants very locally (which there usually are).

Some species and cultivars will berry without pollination (see below). There is really no benefit to the bees in your having female berrying plants, since they do not act as a source of pollen. The blood-red berries are, however, irresistible, especially when contrasted with the dark-green leaves: a wonderful sight on a winter's day, if you can get there before the birds do.

Hollies were commonly used as hedging plants in the past, but their slow growth has caused them to fall from favour. If you have the patience then a holly hedge is a splendid sight and acts as foil for the more brightly coloured plants that might be placed in front of it. It is, however, unlikely to flower if it is clipped annually.

Holly is unfortunately an unreliable source of nectar and pollen; the flowering season is short, at around two–three weeks, and erratic, and in some years virtually non-existent. This may be linked to very low carbohydrate levels in the plant in years following heavy berry crops, and these may take several years to rebuild. This is the hypothesis that has been put forward for the same problem with beech seed crops, and it may well hold good for holly too. Remember that variegated cultivars will need sunnier positions than their green counterparts, and that those cultivars with marginal colouration are more stable and less liable to revert than those with green leaf edges and central leaf colouration.

I x. altaclarensis 'Golden King' Nec. ht: 3.5–4.5m *12–15ft* dist: 3–3.5m *10–12ft.* In spite of its name this cultivar is female and is probably the best and most stable golden variegated holly. Being virtually spineless and easy to handle, it is ideal for wreaths and general decorations. The berries are large, but are not freely produced.

I. aquifolium 'Amber' Nec. ht: 3.5–4.5m *12–15ft* dist: 3–3.5m *10–12ft.* Dark-green shiny leaves with yellow-orange berries carried in tight clusters.

'Handsworth New Silver' Nec. ht: 3.5–4.5m *12–15ft* dist: 3–3.5m *10–12ft.* A purple-stemmed cultivar, leaves dark green with a cream edge; scarlet berries freely produced.

'Golden Queen' Nec./Pol. ht: 3.5–4.5m *12–15ft* dist: 3–3.5m *10–12ft.* A striking cultivar with exceptionally spiny, irregular, golden-margined leaves, the inner areas of these are a mid-green with paler grey shading. The shoots are a dull burgundy with paler pink striations. This is a male cultivar that bears no berries, but it is still an outstanding plant, and useful for both nectar and pollen for the bees.

'J.C. Van Tol' Nec./Pol. ht: 3.5–4.5m *12–15ft* dist: 3–3.5m *10–12ft.* A very free-berrying cultivar with almost spineless dark-green leaves. Berries scarlet.

'Pyramidalis' Nec./Pol. ht: 3.5–4.5m *12–15ft.* An upright cultivar that, like 'J.C. Van Tol', will produce fruit even if it is planted on its own, which suggests that the flowers are either bi-sexual or the berries are produced without fertilisation, in which case they will be seedless. The leaves are virtually spineless, and the scarlet berries are usually freely produced.

'Silver Queen' Nec./Pol. ht: 3.5–4.5m *12–15ft* dist: 3–3.5m *10–12ft*. The leaves are dark green with a cream margin and very spiny. The young leaves are often pinkish cream. No berries.

I. cornuta 'Rotunda' Nec./Pol. ht: 1.25m *4ft* dist: 60–90cm *2–3ft*. Not common in the average garden centre, but worth hunting for if you want a dwarf plant with the most interesting leaf shape of any of the hollies. The leaves are almost rectangular with a narrowed 'waist', and look rather like an animal skin pinned out to dry! The fruits are large and are produced only sparingly, without pollination.

I. crenata 'Golden Gem' Nec. ht: 1m *3ft* dist: 60cm *2ft*. Even slower growing than the previous cultivar, and entirely without spines; leaves yellow, berries black.

Impatiens Nec./Pol. Ann.   ✓
Full sun, shade.
The development of dwarf 'Busy Lizzies' suitable for summer bedding schemes has spiced up the rather staid displays in many a garden or park. They are quite excellent plants and are available in a wide range of glowing colours. They thrive equally well in bright sunshine or the semi-shade into which most British summers deteriorate. The fleshy stems bear attractive toothed leaves. One of the three sepals is modified into a curved spur 3.5cm (1.5in) long, in which nectar is held – quite inaccessible, it might seem. In warm weather, however, the nectar wells to the very top of the spur, where it can be easily extracted by honey bees. There are five flat overlapping petals.

I. novette hybrids ht: 15cm *6in* dist: 23cm *9in* Jun.–Sep. Available in single colours, orange, red, pink, rose, salmon, and mixed. Better weather resistance than other bedding types.

I. glandulifera (Himalayan Balsam, Policeman's Helmet) ht: 1.25–1.15m *4–5ft* dist: 45cm *18in* Jul.–Sep. The flowers of this (and other species naturalised throughout Europe) are quite distinct from the cultivated types and are very freely worked by the honey bees. Appreciable amounts of honey are stored in areas where this plant is abundant. Superficially the flowers resemble those of the Antirrhinum, but the 2.5cm (1in) triangular flower tube is in fact a modified sepal which provides for easy bee access – the bee walks in and then probes for nectar in the downward-pointing green spur. They do this avidly, in spite of the small quantities held there, even on dull cool autumn days, when they emerge covered in white pollen from the mass of anthers in the 'roof' of the flower.

The flowers are quite simply beautiful in form and colour, ranging from white to pink through to purple, with foxglove-like spots and markings both inside and outside the sepal tube. This species, like the others, will thrive equally well in boggy conditions or bone-dry sandy soil in shade. It can be encouraged into the wilder fringes of the garden. After the first touch of frost the fleshy red-green translucent stems collapse, but the plants re-seed themselves freely enough.

✓ 𝒦 **Kniphofia** Nec./Pol. H.
Dry, full sun.
Red-hot-pokers, as Kniphofia is commonly called, are certainly one of the most distinctive of all garden plants, forming great multiple clumps with masses of long narrow leaves. Above the leaves rise the stiffly erect 'pokers', packed tight with masses of individual flowers. The basal flowers always open first, and in many of the older cultivars are a paler colour than the upper ones, giving a two-tone effect, often red above and yellow beneath.

A casual look at the tubular flowers would suggest that the nectar source is inaccessible, but run your hand over the poker-shaped head and it will come away sticky with nectar. So much is in fact produced that it dribbles down the thick stems. This makes them very popular with bees of all sorts, and a number may be seen working the head at the same time.

I can never bring myself to follow the recommended practice of tying the leaves together to help protect the crown of the plant against winter frost and wetness, for the foliage is handsome even in winter, but I have to admit the loss of one or two plants as a consequence. As an alternative, pile some peat or saw-dust around the crown to a depth of 5cm (2in) or so.

Choose your planting site carefully to avoid having to move the plants again for at least four–five years: the roots are thick and fleshy and do not respond well to being disturbed. Kniphofia species are all first-rate 'architectural' plants in the herbaceous or shrub border.

K. caulescens ht: 1m *3ft* dist: 1m *3ft* Sep.–Oct. The broad, blue-green, keeled foliage, rather like *Yucca*, makes this an outstanding species. The dense flower heads are 'traditional' in colour, yellow at the base and red at the tips. Needs some protection in colder areas.

K. galpinii ht: 75cm *2.5ft* dist: 75cm *2.5ft* Sep.–Oct. A neat version of its larger more robust fellows, with orange flowers shading to a pale orange-yellow at their tips. An excellent plant for the autumn garden.

K. northiae ht: 1.25m *4ft* dist: 1.25m *4ft* Aug.–Sep. Grown principally for its bold grey-green foliage, which can be up to 15cm (6in) wide at the base, and 1.25m (4ft) long. Flowers red, ageing to yellow.

K. sparsa syn. *modesta* ht: 60cm *2ft* dist: 60cm *2ft* Jul.–Aug. Neither name sounds terribly promising, but this is a subtly pleasing species, with its pale-pink flower buds opening to an ivory white.

K. uvaria Jun.–Sep. The bulk of the plants offered for sale are derived from this species, which has narrow grey-green keeled leaves, toothed towards the tip. Most will flower for two–three months.

'Bee's Sunset' Flower heads uniformly gold.

'Burnt Orange' ht: 75cm *2.5ft* dist: 75cm *2.5ft*. Flowers pale brown opening to orange.

'Maid of Orleans' ht: 105cm *3.5ft* dist: 105cm *3.5ft*. White flowers.

'Royal Standard' ht: 105cm *3.5ft* dist: 105cm *3.5ft*. The most commonly seen and popular cultivar, with handsome two-tone flower heads of red and yellow.

'Samuel's Sensation' ht: 2m *6ft* dist: 1.5m *5ft*. The giant of the group, with brilliant-red flowers.

Lamium (Deadnettles) Nec./Pol. H.
Semi-shade.

L ✓

The common name is hardly appealing, but it merely means that these are non-stinging types of nettle-like plants.

The leaves of all those mentioned below are coarsely toothed, pungent and are carried on rather lax square-section stems. The flowers are carried in a succession of erect leafy terminal whorls, and even before one has finished flowering the next is ready to take its place. There may be four or five separate flowering 'layers' produced on each stem in a season. The individual flowers may be up to 2.5cm (1in) long and are distinctly two-lipped, the lower broadly two-lobed and serrated. The upper lip, or hood, shelters the flower tube and prevents moisture entering and diluting the nectar.

The four stamens are attached low down on the back of the hood, and the tiny figure-of-eight anthers are usually of a colour that contrasts strongly with the flower: black for the white, and orange or the red wild deadnettles.

Nectar is secreted even on very cold autumn days well into November, or until the flowers are frost-damaged. But it may not always be available to honey bees if the flower tubes are long. It is not uncommon to see the base of the tube holed by bumble-bees in order to get at the nectar, and this also makes access easier for the honey bee. Pollen is also collected, and the wild deadnettle (*L. purpureum*), flowering as early as February, is a useful source at a time when little else is available.

I have never seen the 'weed' types intentionally grown in a garden, but the flowers are beautiful nevertheless. For those who are interested in the conservation of bees in general, the purple deadnettle, *L. purpureum*, and the white deadnettle, *L. album* are two major bumble-bee plants. The latter is probably one of the most nectar-productive of all plants for the amount of space it occupies. So if you can afford the space for a little wild area in your garden these are two plants to encourage.

L. maculatum 'Beacon Silver' ht: 15cm *6in* dist: 23cm *9in* May–Oct. A really striking ground-cover plant with silver, conspicuously net-veined foliage, intermittently spotted with purple. Only the very edges of the leaves are green. The prolific deep-pink flowers sit very prettily atop the grey leaves.

'Shell Pink' ht: 15cm *6in* dist: 30cm *1ft* May–Oct. The leaves have an irregular splash of grey down their centres, and the flowers are a clear shell-pink. There has to be a space for this and the previous cultivar in the smallest of gardens.

L. galeobdolon 'Variegatum' (Yellow Archangel) ht: 30cm *1ft* dist: 60–90cm *2–3ft* May–Jun. A really rampant ground-cover plant that sends out long runners which root at the nodes, smothering any less vigorous plants in its path. I have it planted next to 'Beacon Silver' and 'Shell Pink', and very regular disentangling sessions are required. The leaves are large, up to 10cm (4in) long by 7.5cm (3in) wide, coarsely toothed and irregularly splotched with two broad silver bands. The conspicuous yellow flowers are carried on erect stems. The correct generic name for this plant is now Lamiastrum.

Laurus nobilis (Bay Laurel) Nec. Shr.
ht: 3.5m *12ft* dist: 2.5–3m *8–10ft*
May–Jun., full sun, semi-shade.
This plant is, in Britain at least, rather more interesting as a distinct flavouring for casseroles than as truly decorative garden plant. There is, however, a trend for growing them in pots or tubs, especially for the small town garden, and trimmed to a variety of unusual shapes. In Mediterranean countries these rather easily wind- and frost-damaged plants are commonly clipped into all manner of shapes, usually on a grand scale, as in the Boboli Gardens in Florence. Although the upper parts are subject to frost damage, the roots (as long as they are planted in the ground and not kept in pots) are as tough as old boots, and new shoots are readily produced from them. Left to its own devices, the bay laurel will form a large pyramidal tree.

The masses of inconspicuous yellow-green flowers produce nectar freely during mild weather. If you are interested in having berries (these are shiny, small and black), you must obtain a female plant. The species *angustifolia* has narrower pale-green leaves with wavy edges, and is said to be hardier; *a*. 'Aurea' has leaves of golden yellow. For the evergreen common laurels, see Prunus.

Lavandula (Lavender) Nec./Pol. Shr.   ✓
Jul.–Aug., dry, salt tol., full sun.

The short dark-mauve flowers are carried in several closely tiered heads on long thin stalks, and these are invariably covered with bees during mid-summer. You will know what a good bee plant lavender is when other books warn you not to stick your nose into the flowers for fear of being stung. The grey-green lance-like leaves are also strongly aromatic.

Lavenders look well when mixed with other plants with contrasting leaf shapes, such as Senecio 'Sunshine' and any of the Potentilla species, both of which have yellow flowers that complement the blue of the lavender very well. Dwarf forms can be used in rock gardens or drystone walls. All lavenders tend to become leggy, so trim back the old flower spikes and some of the foliage straight after flowering, taking care not to cut back the stems bare of any green leaves.

Lavenders are common plants in southern Europe, and it is unlikely that you could find a honey from these areas that did not have some lavender in its make-up. It is a major honey plant where it is grown on a field scale.

Lavender

L. augustifolia syn. *officinalis* and *spica*

L. angustifolia syn. *officinalis* and *spica* ht: 60cm *2ft* dist: 45cm *18in*. Sold under a variety of names, but commonly known as 'Old English Lavender'. The most highly scented variety, with lavender-blue flowers.

'Hidcote' syn. 'Nana Atropurpurea' ht: 30cm *1ft* dist: 23–30cm *9–12in*. Silvery leaves, purple flowers. A good dwarf variety.

L. stoechas ht: 60cm *2ft* dist: 45cm *18in*. The French lavender is not entirely hardy, but it is easily raised from collected seed and will produce the odd flower even in its first season. This sounds like a lot of trouble, but it is such a different plant and is so popular with the bees that the effort is worthwhile. The individual flowers, which are deep purple, are packed closely together and topped by three or four paler purple bracts, sticking up just like rabbit's ears. the sub-species *pedunculata* (if you can find it) is even more showy, with paler bracts up to 5cm (2in) long.

✓ **Lavatera** Nec./Pol.
Full sun.
The hardy annuals and herbaceous perennials of this genus are perhaps more seen

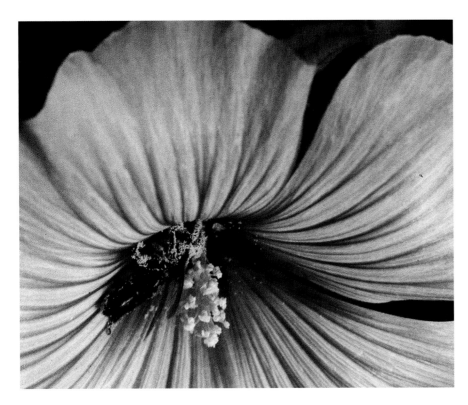

A bee collecting pollen from a Lavatera

in gardens than the shrubs. All, however, have fine glistening satin-like flowers carried in leafy terminal clusters. The stamens, of which there are masses, fan out from a trunk-like base which is fused to the petals. The whole structure looks very like a small frost-laden tree. The cluster of spreading stigmas protruding through the centre of the 'tree' completes the picture. There is white pollen in abundance, so much so that bees working the flowers come away completely covered in it.

L. arborea Shr. ht: 1.25–2m *4–6ft* dist: 60cm *2ft* Aug.–Sep. The tree mallow is often grown as a biennial but will survive in warmer districts and reach 3m (10ft) or so. The flowers are 7.5cm (3in) in diameter, and pale rose-purple. The leaves are softly hairy and may have five–nine lobes.

L. olbia 'Rosea' H. ht: 1–1.25m *3–4ft* dist: 30–45cm *12–18in* Aug.–Sep. Slightly larger reddish-purple flowers, distinctly bi-lobed, petals not quite overlapping as they do in other species. Leaves woolly and three-lobed.

L. trimestris A(h). ht: 30cm *12in* dist: 23cm *9in* Jul.–Oct. The hardy annual mallows have received a lot of attention from the plant breeders over the last few years,

L. vulgaris Privet

and few plants can have repaid this attention so well, the shallow trumpet-shaped flowers being most attractive to the eye. Most grow to about 60cm (2ft).

'Loveliness' Flowers deep rose.

'Mont Blanc' Flowers glistening white.

'Silver Cup' Flowers glowing pink.

Ligustrum (Privet) Nec./Pol. Shr.
Full sun, semi-shade.
A much-derided shrub (or small tree), usually deciduous but evergreen in mild areas. Known to all as a hedging plant and regarded almost universally as the very epitome of all that is worst in a garden plant. There are, however, some very attractive species and cultivars available, especially when they are grown as free-standing shrubs, unpruned, when masses of the small white tubular flowers are carried in erect pyramidal inflorescence, which could be said to have a smell rather than scent. Blackish-purple fruits may follow in some instances, but these are soon taken by birds.

The wheel has turned full circled and the Leyland Cypress, golden or green, which has steadily replaced the privet in so many places, is far more boring than the privet, of which the species *vulgare* is a plant native to much of Europe and very attractive to bees.

Honey from privet is said to have an objectionable smell and to be strongly flavoured, but is unlikely that enough of it is ever made (the privet in flower being a quite uncommon sight) for this to be anything to worry about.

L. ovalifolium 'Aureum' ht: 2.75m *9ft* dist: 2m *6ft* Aug.–Sep. Not as floriferous as the species, but its golden-edged leaves make it such a welcome sight in the dull winter months that perhaps this slight failing can be forgiven, especially since it will be very useful in flower arrangements. In full sun many of the leaves will be almost entirely golden, with only narrow irregular green markings down the main vein.

L. sinense ht: 3–3.5m *10–12ft* dist: 2.5m *8ft* Aug.–Sep. This handsome species has long dense sprays of white flowers and is enthusiastically worked by bees.

✓ **Limnanthes douglasii** Nec./Pol. A(h).
ht: 15cm *6in* dist: 23cm *9in*
May–Sep., full sun.
If you would like a showy white-and-yellow summer carpet, then this is the plant for you. The bees certainly like it. It has been called 'Bee Flower' because honey bees are so attracted to it that it is rarely seen (unless the weather is cold

and wet) without its attendant bees busily collecting both nectar and loads of yellow pollen.

The masses of slightly cupped, sweetly scented flowers have five shallowly notched petals and are white, 2.6cm (1in) across, with a very prominent yellow eye. Its common name, Poached or Fried Egg Plant, is an apt one. The much-divided leaves are yellowish-green, and the rather weak stems give the whole plant a straggling habit. Its natural habitat is damp marshy areas, but it will grow without too much trouble even in dry soil. Once you have grown Limnanthes you will never be without it – it seeds down readily and appears year after year, gradually spreading, unless checked.

Linaria (Toadflax) Nec./Pol.
Jun.–Oct., full sun.
The flower structure, if not the name, will be familiar to all, since it is very similar to that of Antirrhinum with its 'Snapdragon' closed lips. The lower lip of the flower may be a similar or contrasting colour. But, unlike Antirrhinum, the very pretty flowers are small enough for the honey bee's weight to open them, so access can be gained to the nectar and pollen. This is held in a 1.3cm (0.5in) narrow tapering 'horn', and during warm weather it will build up to a sufficient height for some of the excess to be drawn off. There are now open-flowered types of Antirrhinum that allow honey bees access for nectar and pollen.

L. douglasii, Poached or Fried Egg Plant is sometimes called Meadow Foam and is a prolific plant loved by bees

L. alpina (Alpine Toadflax) A(h). ht: 7.5cm *3in* dist: 23cm *9in*. Purple-blue flowers with an orange lip and fleshy grey-green foliage. It will grow in the poorest of soils as long as it has sun. Ideal for the rock garden, where it will usually seed itself quite happily.

L. maroccana 'Excelsior' A(h). ht: 30cm *12in* dist: 23cm *9in*. Wide range of colours in shades of yellow, pink, blue, red and purple.

'Fairy Bouquet' A(h). ht: 23cm *9in* dist: 15–23cm *6–9in*. Wide colour range as above. Both these cultivars should be sown in situ in March or April in association with other annuals, or at the front of herbaceous or shrub borders.

L. prupurea H. ht: 90cm *3ft* dist: 60cm *2ft*. Flowers bluish-purple with a white bearded mouth.

L. vulgaris (Common Toadflax) H. ht: 30–60cm *1–2ft* dist: 23cm *9in*. The flowers are a sulphury yellow with an orange lip and striated spur. In common with many other hedgerow plants, the widely distributed common toadflax, found throughout Europe (except in Portugal), has made something of a comeback in recent years, due to the reduced frequency of verge mowing.

✓ **Lithodora** (syn. **Lithospermum**) *diffusum*
'Heavenly Blue' Nec. Shr.
ht: 60cm *2ft* dist: 60–120cm *2–4ft*
Apr.–Jul., acid, dry, full sun, semi-shade.
This is a jewel of a plant. To see sheets of it in the wild, cascading over rocks like a blue waterfall, is a sight once seen never forgotten. It will also grow perfectly well on the flat, and it is a rampant grower needing to be restrained annually, although it rarely exceeds 15–23cm (6–9in) in height. The lance-shaped to oval leaves are dark green above, paler beneath, up to 2.5cm (1in) long and covered with short stiff hairs. The leaf margins are rolled downwards. The small flowers are carried in terminal clusters, and have five broadly rounded petals which narrow suddenly to a tube, 8mm (0.33in) or so in length. The petals are gentian blue, and the tube tends more towards a purplish blue. The tube might be thought rather long for bees, but it does fill with nectar and is a real favourite with them.

L. oleifolium ht: 30cm *12in* dist: 30–45cm *12–18in* Jun.–Sep. Leaves larger and broader than the previous species, silkily hairy beneath. The more open, bell-shaped pale blue flowers allow easy access for bees. More tender than 'Heavenly Blue'.

Lobelia Nec. Ann.
ht: 15cm *6in* dist: 23cm *9in*
May–Oct., full sun.
These are best known as dwarf, blue, summer-flowering bedding plants (see *erinus* below), often used in conjunction with Lobularia – one white one, one blue one, one white one, and so on. There are some striking erect herbaceous species (and a few evergreen shrubs), but unfortunately most of these have flower tubes too long for the honey bee.

L. erinus ht: 15cm *6in* dist: 15–23cm *6–9in* May–Oct.. The pale-blue flowers are distinctly two-lipped: two narrow lobes above and three rather broad ones below (rather like the Marsh Orchid), with a white or yellowish eye. The flowers stud the domed plants right through to the first frosts. A large number of cultivars are available, all virtually the same except for the flower colour.

'Blue Pearl' Deep-blue flowers with a small white eye.

'Crystal Palace' Deep-blue flowers, with the added attraction of purplish-bronze foliage.

'Rosamund' Showy carmine flowers with white eye.

'Blue Cascade', 'Sapphire' and 'Red Cascade' are trailing cultivars, but are only really suitable for use in window boxes or hanging baskets, or for cascading over drystone walls or rocks.

Lobularia maritima syn. **Alyssum maritima** (Sweet Alyssum) Nec./Pol. A(h).
ht: 15cm *6in* dist: 15cm *6in*
May–Oct., dry, salt tol., full sun.
The 'other half' of the blue-and-white edging that forms such a well-known part of so many summer bedding schemes. Now, in addition to white there is a wide range of flower colours available, all producing masses of fragrant, typically small cruciferous flowers in rounded heads, which provide large quantities of both nectar and pollen. It is a superb cultivar with its rosy-red flowers. Pink, lilac and purple-flowered cultivars are also available. The seed may be sown in March or April where it is to flower, and the plants thrive on the poorest and driest of soils.

Lonicera (Honeysuckle) Nec./Pol. Shr.
Full sun, semi-shade.

Lonicera *x purpusii* Honeysuckle

The climbing Loniceras, with their marvellously fragrant long tubular flowers, so well adapted for the long tongues of moths and butterflies but so inaccessible to bees, immediately spring to mind whenever the honeysuckles are mentioned. This genus is, however, far more variable than most people imagine, and it also boasts some excellent deciduous and evergreen non-climbing shrubs. The flowers vary enormously in size, depending on species, and are carried in pairs in the shrubby species, the climbers have terminal or axillary clusters.

CLIMBERS

L. japonica ht: 4.5m *15ft* Jun.–Oct. The only climbing honeysuckle with flower tubes short enough for bees to extract nectar. A vigorous evergreen or semi-evergreen species with short 2.5cm (1in) flowers, white at first, changing to yellow as they age. Not particularly showy but a fast grower and the fragrance is delicious. The cultivar 'Aureoreticulata', with yellow leaf venation, is a beautiful plant, but unfortunately it rarely bears any flowers.

SHRUBS

L. fragrantissima ht: 2m *6ft* dist: 2m *6ft* Feb.–Apr. Semi-evergreen with small, 1.3cm (0.5in) fragrant creamy flowers carried on the semi-naked branches in late winter and spring. The species *standishii* is similar, *x purpusii* (the result of a union between *fragrantissima* and *standishii*) is slightly less vigorous but otherwise very similar.

L. involucrata syn. *ledebourii* ht: 2.5m *8ft* dist: 2.5m *8ft* Jun.–Jul. A robust leafy shrub, definitely not everyone's cup of tea, but the yellow flowers are carried in large numbers and upon close inspection are very attractive, surrounded as they are by two conspicuous rather waxy red bracts. These persist and contrast nicely with the small black fruits.

L. syringantha ht: 1.5m *5ft* dist: 1.5m *5ft* May–Jun. A rather slow-growing, stiff yet arching shrub with 1.3cm (0.75in) fragrant tubular flowers of a soft lilac.

L. tatarica ht: 2.75m *9ft* dist: 2.75m *9ft* May–Jun. Produces masses of pink flowers which are followed by red berries.

Evergreen honeysuckles such as *nitida* and *pileata* tend to be grown more as trimmed hedges than specimens in their own right. They do not flower freely in cool climates and clipping them ensures they have little chance of ever doing so.

Lysimachia (Loosestrife) Nec./Pol. H.
The three species described are so different from each other that you could be forgiven for thinking they were from separate genera.

L. clethroides ht: 90cm *3ft* dist: 60cm *2ft* Aug.–Oct., full sun, semi-shade. The long 'kinked' white flower heads look rather like those of the more graceful of the hebes, and give this plant its common name 'Gooseneck Loosestrife'. A splendid rhizomatous clump-forming plant with good autumn tints that is certainly not planted as widely as it deserves to be.

L. nummularia (Creeping Jenny) ht: 7.5cm *3in* dist: 45cm *18in* Jul.–Aug., full sun, semi-shade. A real spreader, with branched creeping stems clothed with opposite rounded leaves. The erect, bright-yellow, slightly cupped flowers, 2cm (0.75in) across, are freely produced, one from each leaf axil. Planted next to more vigorous plants its invasive nature will be curbed. The golden-leaved form 'Aurea' is very attractive, but flowers less freely.

L. punctata ht: 90cm *3ft* dist: 60cm *2ft* Jul.–Aug., full sun, shade. A rather stiff unbranched plant with leaves opposite or in whorls, lance-shaped with hairy margins. Numerous yellow flowers, 2cm (0.75in) in diameter, carried in the leaf axils. Each whorl flowers at the same time, producing a mass of 90cm (3ft) yellow spikes. The eye is slightly darker than the ground-colour of the flower.

This is the most invasive of the three species, requiring a firm hand at the end of each growing season. It is often quite well established in the wild, in ditches and woodland throughout Europe.

Lythrum (Purple Loosestrife) Nec./Pol. H.
Jun.–Oct., wet, full sun, semi-shade.
The purple loosestrife is now rarely seen in cultivation. It is, however, a splendid

sight growing wild in great clumps by the riverside, the 30cm (1ft) long rose-purple flower spikes held stiffly erect, and how well it looks with that other native of damp places, the creamy Meadowsweet.

Although it prefers damp conditions, it will do well enough in any good soil that is reasonably moisture-retentive. The bright six-petalled purple or pink propeller-like flowers are about 2.5cm (1in) in diameter, and have lemon-green stamens. These are of three different lengths, and produce three different sizes of pollen grains – the shorter the stamen the smaller the grain – a most unusual feature. An excellent bee plant for nectar and pollen for summer and autumn.

L. salicaria 'Firecandle' ht: 60–90cm *2–3ft* dist: 45m *18in.* Flowers intense rose-red.

'Robert' ht: 45–60cm *18–24in* dist: 45cm *18in.* Flowers bright pink.

L. virgatum 'Rose Queen' ht: 45cm *18in* dist: 30cm *12in.* Bright rose-red, but the flower spikes are less robust than the other species.

Magnolia Pol. Shr.
Acid, full sun, semi-shade.
I never really understood why people raved about Magnolias until I had seen the beautiful lily-shaped flowers of *M. denudata* (Lily Tree), standing erect in rows on naked horizontal branches, for all the world like pure-white pine cones. The plant in question was some 4.5m (15ft) high, set in a sheltered semi-woodland setting, and the spring sky was blue. Being in the South West of England, the waxy flowers of this and other Magnolias were not often damaged by frosts, as they are so commonly in colder climes. Most keen gardeners are prepared to risk frost damage for the one year in three to five when no flower damage occurs. Keen beekeepers, however, may not be so tolerant of a plant that, in Britain at least, appears to yield pollen only.

The majority of Magnolias are far too large for the average garden, and only relatively small species are mentioned here. All Magnolias benefit from being sheltered from cold winds in spring.

M. liliiflora ht: 2.75m *9ft* dist: 2.25–2.5m *7–8ft* Apr.–Jun. Flowers erect, with a purple flush on the outside of the petals, eventually opening to reveal a creamy-white interior.

'Nigra' ht: 2.25–2.5m *7–8ft* dist: 2m *6ft* Apr.–Jun. Darker purple exterior to the petals, white inside with purple staining. Rather more compact than the species.

M. x soulangeana ht: 3.5m *12ft* dist: 3–3.5m *10–12ft* Apr.–May. Many cultivars of this vigorous species, with wide spreading branches, are seen in cultivation.

Magnolia *x soulangeana* var. *Alexandrina*

The large flowers are tulip-shaped, and white with purplish staining at their bases. It is more tolerant of lime than many species, and seen in combination with yews (as in churchyards) it is a marvellous sight when in full flower.

M. stellata (Star Magnolia ht: 1.5–2.25m *5–7ft* dist: 2m *6ft* Mar–Apr. A fabulous plant, slow growing like all Magnolias, but well worth the wait to see a bush covered with the starry flowers, each composed of sixteen narrow petals. The fragrant flowers are in fact much more resistant to frost and wind damage than any of the other cultivars or species I am familiar with. The grey hairy winter buds are an attractive feature.

Pink-flowered cultivars 'Rosea' and 'Rubra' may also be available in good garden centres.

✓ **Mahonia** Nec./Pol. Shr.
Full sun, semi-shade.
No garden should be without at least one of these handsome evergreens, with their glossy, dark-green, pinnately-divided leaves, which can be up to 60cm (2ft) long and often take on beautiful red tints during the winter months. The new growth also takes on pinky-red colouration in spring. Individual leaflets, which are pale beneath, are holly-like in shape, size and prickliness.

The flowers are the crowning glory, deep-primrose in colour, 8mm (0.33in) in diameter, produced in long or short terminal or axillary clusters and most deliciously scented – reminiscent of lily-of-the-valley. These are followed in all species by clusters of small, bloomy, blue-black fruits, which are

Magnolia *x soulangeana* var. *Wigra*

usually quickly taken by birds, with the consequence that the fully developed fruits are rarely seen.

The six stamens are inserted into shallow depressions at the base of each petal and it is here that the nectar collects, and exceedingly sweet it is too. The flowers are extremely attractive to honey bees, and the flowering time makes it a very useful plant to fill in periods when other forage flowers are scarce especially in a suburban district where oil-seed rape is absent.

M. aquifolium (Oregon Grape) ht: 1.25–1.5m *4–5ft* dist: 1–2.25m *3–7ft* Mar.–May. By far the most common species seen in cultivation, but fast being replaced by more exotic cultivars. The rich yellow flower spikes are short and are carried both terminally and in the leaf axils. The leaves are in scale with the flowers, and can be very highly coloured – including the leaf stalks and veins in winter. Very easily grown, this plant will tolerate quite dense shade and can be hacked back to ground level if it becomes overwhelming or too antisocial!

The cultivar 'Atropurpurea' has even darker red-purple leaves in winter.

M. x media 'Charity' ht: 2m *6ft* dist: 1.5–2m *5–6ft* Dec.–Mar. A really bold plant, with its 60cm (2ft) rather pointed leaves and long erect terminal flower spikes carried over a much longer period than any other cultivar.

M. japonica ht: 2m *6ft* dist: 1.5–2m *5–6ft* Jan.–Mar. Like *x media* 'Charity', the leaves are large and handsome but the rather lax pale-primrose flower spikes are far more elegant. A superb plant.

There are many other species and cultivars, all of which are suitable for garden use since none of them bears double flowers.

Mahonias look well mixed with deciduous plants to give contrast or as specimens amongst lower growing ground-cover plants. If they do become too large then they may be cut back very hard, and this will encourage new shoots to be produced from the base. It is best to phase such pruning over a four-year period so that the plant continues to flower right through the exercise.

✓ **Malus** (Eating and Crab-Apples Nec./Pol. T.
Apr.–May, full sun.
Apples can be grown in the relatively sunny and dry areas of Britain and in more northern and wetter areas, and there are early and mid-season cultivars (as opposed to late), which make a showing under these conditions. Diseases to be aware of are canker, collar rot and scab.

Unlike many other plants, apples need to be cross-pollinated by another cultivar in order to produce good crops of fruit. For this to happen they must flower at around the same time. Some cultivars, such as 'Bramley's Seedling', produce pollen which is useless for pollination, so if growing this cultivar two other cultivars are needed to ensure pollination of the Bramley and of each other. Usually, however, there will be sufficient pollinators (and these can be crab-apples) in suburban areas to ensure reasonable pollination without having to devote space to a second or third cultivar that you may not want. The flowers are quite open and the nectar readily available to the bees, but it is also easily diluted by rain or heavy dews, reducing the sugar concentration to a level at which bees are not attracted.

For most small to average-sized gardens select your cultivars, grafted or budded, on dwarfing rootstocks such as M27, or semi-dwarfing such as M26, or the slightly more vigorous M9. This will ensure that your trees do not grow to enormous proportions, as many of them are capable of doing on more vigorous rootstocks. The choice of the form of the tree will be up to the individual, but where space is restricted the single-stemmed cordon, the flat-tiered espalier or aptly named fan are very suitable, especially where less vigorous rootstocks are used.

Buy your trees ready trained unless you have lots of patience and a good deal of expertise! Crab-applies will not be trained, but still try to ensure that you have some idea of the ultimate size of the tree, which will depend on the rootstock: MM106 will give a larger tree than any of the rootstocks previously listed. Avoid the rootstock M9 for crab-apples, since trees grown on it will require permanent staking, which is acceptable for a 'cropping' tree but not for an ornamental one.

There is a host of other cultivators to tempt you, but try to taste the fruit before committing yourself for the next twenty years or so. If you really must try something different, then consider one of the so-called 'family trees', which have several cultivars on one rootstock.

Fruit-tree pruning is far too big a subject to deal with here, but try to prune every year, if only to thin crowded or crossing branches.

CRAB-APPLES

M. floribunda (Japanese Crab) ht: 4.5m *15ft* Apr. A real toffee-apple shaped tree, often wider than it is high, also very suitably grown as a shrub. The crimson buds which crown the arching branches open to a pinkish white and never fail, regardless of the season, to give a fabulous display. The fruits are not very showy.

'Golden Hornet' ht: 4.5m *15ft* Apr. White flowers followed by an abundance of yellow fruits that persist well into the new year.

'John Downie' ht: 4.5m *15ft* Apr. Justifiably regarded as the best of the fruiting crabs, at least as far as its edible, bright orange-red conical fruits are concerned. The flowers are white.

'Profusion' ht: 5.5m *28ft* Apr. The large wine-red and fragrant flowers are produced as the name suggests. The young leaves are purplish but change to coppery red, which complements the small deep-red fruits perfectly; the fruit colour is more than skin deep and they look delicious – but are not.

'Red Jade' ht: 3.5m *12ft* May. So named on account of its very persistent brilliantly red fruits, which follow the pink-white flowers.

M. sargentii ht: 3m *9ft* Apr. This species is really more suitably grown as a shrub. The leaves are often distinctly three-lobed, and the flowers white with golden anthers. Very free-flowering. The bees love it and can be seen working the flowers in great number. Fruit bright red and cherry-like.

DESSERT AND CULINARY APPLES

If grown as cordons, space these at 75cm (2.5ft), and if as fans or espaliers at 2–2.5m (6–8ft).

'Cox's Orange Pippin' This dessert apple does not do well under wet, relatively sunless conditions.

'Malling Kent' A possible alternative to Cox, and heavier cropping, less fussy and much easier to grow.

'Spartan' The dark-red skin polishes to a mirror-like shine and the white flesh tinged with green is as good to look at as it is to eat. It stores well, but like most cultivars is best eaten straight off the tree.

'Bramley's Seedling' There can be no argument over the fact that this is the finest culinary apple, and it is also a more than passable eater if stored. It tends to be rather vigorous, even on dwarfing rootstocks, so is best not grown as a cordon. The fruits are large and green, and some reddish-orange colouration is often present. The fruits store exceptionally well. Remember that if you decide you need pollinators, two will be required.

Malva Nec./Pol. H.
ht: 90cm *3ft* dist: 60cm *2ft*
Jun.–Oct., full sun.
A common name shared by two different genera of plants would suggest a fairly close botanical relationship. The marked visual similarity between species of Malva and Lavatera – both known as mallows – reinforces this, and with their masses of pollen both are equally attractive to the honey bee. Malva pollen is white, and the grains are some of the very largest known, having a diameter in excess of 1mm: clearly visible to the naked eye.

Several species are found in the wild and some, such as *moschata* (Musk Mallow) are native to most of Europe. All are very easy to grow.

M. alcea Pink flowers 5–7.5cm (2–3in) across, leaves rounded at the base and variably divided above. The more upright form 'Fastigiata', which grows to 1.2m (4ft), is now frequently offered by seedsmen.

M. moschata Bright rose-purple flowers, up to 5cm (2in) in diameter. The leaves of this species are an added attraction, being deeply divided, rather like those of the cranesbills. The popular form 'Alba' has glistening white flowers and can be raised from seed.

Meconopsis Nec./Pol.
Semi-shade.
Botanically the Meconopsis genus is nearly related to the poppies which they closely resemble. They do, however, need rather different growing conditions. A well-drained soil with a good organic content and partial shelter is essential if they are to thrive.

M. betonicifolia (Himalayan Poppy) Bien. ht: 90cm *3ft* dist: 45cm *18in* Jun.–Jul., acid. Once seen, these tall, brilliant-blue poppies with their masses of yellow stamens are never forgotten. The mind's eye transports them immediately to some Tibetan hillside which is their true home.

The individual flowers may be up to 6.5cm (2.5in) in diameter, and there are usually several on each stem. The greyish-green leaves have very long stalks, 20–23cm (8–9in), with a 7.5–10cm (3–4in) elliptic to oblong leaf blade which has flat notched lobes, not at all typical of the poppy family. Strictly speaking this species is perennial, but it is rather short-lived, so treat it as a biennial (see *M. regia* for details).

M. cambrica (Welsh Poppy) Bien. ht: 30cm *1ft* dist: 23cm *9in* Jun.–Sep. This species has seeded itself around the British countryside and gardens. The 3.5cm (1.5in) yellow flowers are very fine. There is an orange form, 'Aurantiaca'.

M. grandis H. ht: 60cm *2ft* dist: 30cm *1ft* May–Jun. Variable but mostly blue flowers up to 10cm (4in) in diameter. The cultivar 'Branklyn' has more reliably blue flowers.

M. regia Bien. ht: 1.5m *5ft* dist: 60cm *2ft* May–Jun. The large yellow flowers are very showy, as are the magnificent 60cm (2ft) densely silver- or golden-haired, typical poppy-like leaves. Usually dies after flowering, so new plants should be raised each year.

Seed of all the species listed above, and many others, is available from a number of seed firms. Good news for the bees, which work the flowers so avidly.

Melissa (Bee Balm) Nec./Pol. H.
Jun.–Sep., semi-shade.
The white flowers are generally regarded as having too long a corolla tube for them to provide an easy nectar source for the honey bee, so it is not grown on this account alone, but on another.

The crinkly, scalloped nettle-like leaves are not only attractive, particularly in their yellow-green form, but they also have the most delicious lemon scent. Bee Balm was used by the ancient skep beekeepers to rub on the inside of empty skeps to attract passing honey bee swarms into them – the original 'bait hives'. It has been shown that the aromatic scents of the balm plant are the same as, or very similar to, those in Nasonov pheromone, which is fanned by the wings from a gland at the end of the abdomen and attracts other bees; it is used to collect stragglers and to guide the swarm into its new home. The ancient technique is, therefore, based on keen observation, and no doubt had some success.

M. officinalis 'Aurea' ht: 45cm *18in* dist: 30cm *12in*. Golden leaves, continuous from spring to first frosts. Some light shade helps to prevent scorching of the foliage.

'Variegata' ht: 60cm *2ft* dist: 45cm *18in*. Golden and green mottled leaves. No herb garden (or herbaceous border) should be without this superb plant.

Mentha (Mint) Nec. H.
Aug.–Oct., full sun, semi-shade.
The flavour and fragrance of the various mints are universally known, but unfortunately it rarely grows in sufficient quantity, in any of its forms, to yield a large amount of the deliciously mint-flavoured honey.

The small four-lobed tubular flowers are carried in dense whorls, each flower enclosed at its base by a conspicuously veined and hairy five-pointed calyx.

In spite of their small size the flowers produce large quantities of nectar and are a particularly valuable late summer source. Unfortunately, the flowers are all too rarely seen in cultivation, the new growths being picked for various

Melissa *officinalis*

✓

flavourings well before they reach the nectar stage. The more ornamental forms, with crinkly or variegated foliage, which are not normally used for flavouring, ironically produce very little in the way of flower. There are, however, many wild forms (and hybrids thereof) that flower freely, mostly in damp semi-shaded areas.

Many of the mints are invasive and are often contained by planting in bottom-less buckets or pipes, sunk to their rims to prevent the runners from spreading too much. You could use more vigorous neighbouring plants to help cure your mint's exuberance, but unless there is plenty of moisture in the soil the mint could end up suffering badly.

M. gentilis 'Variegata' (Ginger Mint) ht: 45cm *18in* dist: 30–45cm *12–18in*. Nettle-like leaves heavily veined with gold, dark-red stems and pale-lilac flowers.

M. pulegium (Penny Royal) ht: 23cm *9in* dist: 30–45cm *12–18in*. A good ground-cover plant, with small, shiny green leaves. Freely produced lavender-coloured flowers. The whole plant is strongly aromatic.

✓ **Muscari** (Grape Hyacinth) Nec./Pol. B./C.
ht: 12.5–23cm *5–9in* dist: 10–15cm *4–6in*
Mar.–May, full sun, semi-shade.
Muscari have a long flowering season and manage not only to look after themselves but also to extend their territory, even onto hard-packed gravel paths. This ability to grow virtually anywhere is perhaps less commonly seen now that persistent weedkillers are used so widely on paths and other 'odd corners'. The flower spikes are crowded with small, blue bell-shaped flowers 8 x 6mm (0.33 x 0.25in), with a narrow petticoat of white around their fluted edges. The strong blue of Muscari looks well with dwarf narcissus and/or primroses. Growing near and through a dwarf white-flowered variegated Arabis, this makes an attractive combination and gives dual interest for the bees. In fact, the plant appears to be much more attractive to honey bees than you might expect from its size and shape.

If you are worried about them spreading too much, cut off the flower spikes well before the seed is shed. Otherwise you have the bonus of the dried silvery-brown flower spikes, rather like small versions of Honesty, right through the winter. The flower scent is not unpleasant, but could be described as an acquired taste. Plant the bulbs about 7.5cm (3in) deep.

M. armeniacum Bright-blue flowers on long spikes. The grass-like foliage is produced in autumn, long before the flower spikes. It can be invasive and will in time smother less vigorous alpines. Dwarf forms such as 'Cantab' may be available from specialist producers.

M. azureum A softer, paler blue than other species.

M. botryoides Not highly rated by most gardeners, but its larger, more globular-shaped flowers make it a worthwhile addition. Not widely available, but it should prove easy enough to 'borrow' a few to get you started. The white form, *album*, which is less vigorous, is commonly grown on the rock garden.

Nemophila menziesii Nec. A(h).
ht: 15–20cm *6–8in* dist: 23cm *9in*
Full sun, semi-shade.
This is better known by its common name, 'Baby Blue Eyes'. The eye of the shallow, five-petalled, sky-blue flowers is in fact white. The stems are lax, and bear 5cm (2in) long leaves which are divided virtually to the central vein. A very pleasant little plant, and quite attractive to bees, who forage for nectar and pollen, coming away with blue-grey loads on their legs.

Nepeta (Catmint or Catnip) Nec./Pol. H.
Jun.–Sep., dry, full sun.
If you already have catmint in your garden and would like to know its correct generic or cultivar name, you may have problems. The nomenclature seems to be rather confused, and there is no doubt that there are a fair number of seed-raised hybrids around, often self-sown, that have found their way into cultivation, thus adding to the confusion. All the plants that I have seen are equally attractive to bees, there being literally hundreds of individual two-lipped flowers on even a small plant.

Cats adore the smell and will devastate your plants by chewing, scratching and rolling all over them, and will return for a regular fix! Catmints are, however, pretty tough and will usually win through. Most people find the smell verging on the offensive, but if you do not get too close you cannot fail to be won over by its very long flowering season and pretty blue flowers carried on

Nepeta Catmint or Catnip. Bees appreciate it too

long spikes, complemented by grey or green toothed leaves. An excellent bee plant. Tidy by cutting down to ground level in the autumn.

N. x faassenii ht: 45cm *18in* dist: 60cm *2ft.* Leaves grey and downy, flowers pale lavender. Does not produce seed.

N. gigantean 'Six Hills Giant' ht: 75–90cm *2.5–3ft* dist: 90cm *3ft.* An altogether more vigorous plant; leaves greener and flowers violet-blue, lower lip frilled and spotted.

Nigella damascena (Love-in-a-Mist) Nec./Pol. A(h).
ht: 45cm *18in* dist: 23cm *9in*
Jun.–Oct., full sun.
The common name most aptly describes the impression given by this rather elegant plant, with its feathery leaves and epicalyxes surrounding the solitary terminal flowers. As the buds open, the 'ruff' is pushed outwards to reveal the five or six pointed petals. The flower really is quite beautiful and has a mass of stamens from which emerge five or six writhing pistils. The dozen or so nectaries, which sit at the base of the petals, look rather like a black cow's head with two dark shiny eyes and a long nose, complete with eyebrows and nasal hair! The 'nose' separates to give access to the bag-like nectar store, which is well protected from the elements.

Seed is usually sown in situ in March, and dwarf cultivars are available. When the flowers are over, the inflated seed pods dry very well and are frequently seen in winter flower arrangements.

'Miss Jekyll' Cornflower blue.

'Persian Jewels' An interesting mixture of blue, mauve, purple, pink and white flowers.

Oenothera (Evening Primrose) Pol.
Jun.–Sep., dry, full sun.
In spite of their common name most of the species open their flowers by day. Pollination, however, is not achieved until the evening, when long-tongued moths take the nectar from the deep narrow flower tube into which the four rather flat petals are fused, and all are yellow unless otherwise stated. The sepals, which are fused with the flower tube, are often of a different colour, frequently dull red or pink. It is not uncommon to see Oenothera naturalised by the roadside, particularly on waste or recently disturbed ground, and they do make ideal plants for a hot dry location.

The pollen grain of Oenothera is shaped like a 'Y', with equal-length limbs and angles, and it also has several long threads growing from the centre part of the grain. Honey bees work the flowers for pollen, but find it almost impossible to pack it in their 'pollen baskets', at least tidily, so one sees them coming away from the plant trailing a ribbon of tangled pollen grains from their legs.

O. biennis (Evening Primrose) Bien. ht: 90cm *3ft* dist: 60cm *2ft* Jun.–Sep. 'The' evening primrose. Flowers 3.5cm (1.5in) across on slender spikes.

O. caespitosa H. ht: 15cm *6in* dist: 30cm *12in* Jun.–Sep. One for the rock garden or scree bed. Pure-white flowers 6.5cm (2.5in) across.

O. missouriensis H. ht: 23cm *9in* dist: 30–45cm *12–18in.* The shallow bowl-shaped flowers, 10cm (4in) across, are quite superb on this rather dwarf sprawling plant. Waxy leaves.

O. tetragona 'Fireworks' H. ht: 45cm *18in* dist: 30cm *12in* Jun.–Sep. A very colourful plant with purplish leaves and red flower buds.

Olearia (Daisy Bush) Nec./Pol. Shr.
Dry, salt tol., full sun.
What an apt common name this is for these most easily grown Australasian shrubs, which thrive in dry soils and tolerate any amount of sun. In season they are literally smothered with the white, many-petalled, single chrysanthemum-like flowers. The leaves are usually grey or grey-green and quite leathery. They are unfortunately not reliably hardy except in milder coastal districts, so if you live inland and wish to preserve your stock, take a few of the easily rooted cuttings each year in August, or you will probably lose your plants about one year in four or five, but they do grow quickly.

O. x haastii ht: 2m *6ft* dist: 1.25–1.5m *4–5ft* Jun.–Jul. By far the hardiest, and worth trying even in cold areas. The fragrant flowers are produced very freely, leaves dark green above, grey-felted beneath.

O. macrodonta ht: 2.5m *8ft* dist: 2–2.5m *6–7ft* Jun.–Jul. Handsome sage-green holly-like leaves, silvery-white-felted beneath. Masses of fragrant flowers carried in rounded 15cm (6in) clusters.

Origanum (Marjoram) Nec./Pol.   ✓
Full sun.
Best known for its culinary properties, there are also some very ornamental species, all of which produce nectar copiously from the small distinctly two-lipped flowers. The flowers of all species have tubular bases, but many of the most ornamental ones are far too long for honey bees to penetrate, so care must be taken when choosing your plants.

O. marjorana (Sweet or Knotted Marjoram) Ann. ht: 60m *2ft* dist:45cm *18in* Jul.–Sep. This is best treated as an annual in the British climate, although strictly speaking it is a perennial. The leaves are strongly aromatic and this is 'the' marjoram for cooking purposes. Remember that if you use too many shoots or leaves, the flowers (inconspicuous but very attractive to bees) will be few and far between.

O. rotundifolium H. ht: 23cm *9in* dist: 45cm *18in* Aug.–Oct. Glaucous leaves and pink flowers almost obscured by the drooping clusters of pale-green, hop-like bracts. Not reliably hardy.

O. vulgare H. ht: 30cm *12in* dist: 30cm *12in* Jul.–Sep. In spite of its name this is a very attractive plant, especially in the wild, growing in short grass in any dryish soil throughout Europe. It is worked very enthusiastically by bees.

The flower stems are reddish, as are the buds in the clustered flower heads before they open to white. There is always a good mixture of buds and flowers, making this a very pretty plant indeed. In the wild, on the alkaline soils where this plant is plentiful, its nectar is converted into a strong mint-flavoured honey which is delicious. Unfortunately, as with many of the plant essential oils, the fine aromatic flavour of Marjoram honey will only be found when freshly extracted, as it is lost during crystallisation.

Osmanthus Nec./Pol. Shr.
Full sun.
The clusters of small, white, four-petalled flowers are not particularly striking, but are plentiful and show up well against the dark evergreen leaves, and they are beautifully scented, rather reminiscent of Jasmine.

O. delavayi ht: 2.25m *7ft* dist: 2.25m *7ft* Apr.–May. By far the most commonly planted species, with finely toothed leaves.

O. heterophyllus ht: 3m *10ft* dist: 2.5–3m *8–10ft* Sep.–Oct. Rather variable, prickly, holly-like leaves which may be up to 7.5cm (3in) long. The golden and white variegated forms, 'Aureomarginatus' and 'Variegatus' respectively, are both showy and, as with all such plants, are slower growing.

Papaver (Poppy) Pol.
Full sun.
Although the cornfield poppy is most familiar, the genus does, however, contain many other species, large and small, annual and perennial, in a wide range of very showy colours, all of which (with the exception of double-flowered cultivars) bear large amounts of pollen. This is blue-black in the field poppy, but usually greenish-yellow in other species. Poppy pollen is extremely attractive to the honey bee, which will search out the flowers wherever they occur. The mass

of stamens surround a barrel-shaped pistil surmounted by a large ribbed stigma. The whole structure swells to become the familiar poppy seed head, which is so widely used in dried-flower arrangements.

There are usually four or six petals of a satiny texture, and as they are unsupported by sepals (which fall early) they are in constant motion in even the slightest breeze. Most poppies seed themselves very freely, so unless you are prepared for an invasion cut the seed heads off before they have time to mature. The foliage is variable but is usually much divided and in some species hairy.

P. alpinum H. ht: 23cm *9in* dist: 23cm *9in* May–Aug. Flowers usually bright yellow (but white, pink and orange forms also occur), and up to 3.5cm (1.5in) in diameter. The leaves are blue-green and much divided. A marvellous little alpine plant for the rock garden or scree.

P. commutatum 'Ladybird' A(h). ht: 45cm *18in* dist: 23cm *9in* Jun.–Oct. A real show-stopper, with brilliant red petals each of which has a jet-black spot.

P. nudicaule (Iceland Poppy) Bien. ht: 60cm *2ft* dist: 45cm *18in* Jun.–Oct. These large, 6.5cm (2.5in), fragrant flowers have a fabulous pastel colour range. The cultivar 'Champagne Bubbles' is rather less vigorous and has attractively crinkled petals. Although it is a perennial it is not a long-lived one, so is best treated as an annual or biennial. It is also the only poppy suitable for use as a cut flower, since it does not drop its petals as freely as other species. Plant them at the edges of borders of herbaceous plants or other annuals.

P. orientale H. May–Jun. The giant of the group, both with regard to height and its massive 15cm (6in) flowers – a statuesque and very showy plant. The leaves are long, dark green and bristly. Unless they are grown in good light, without shade, the flowering stems will need some support, but this weakness can be overcome to a certain extent by choosing one of the less vigorous cultivars. Ideal plants for the mixed shrub or herbaceous border.

'Allegro' ht: 45cm *18in* dist: 45–60cm *18–24in*. Scarlet flowers on short stems.

'Goliath' ht: 1.25m *4ft* dist: 1m *3ft*. Scarlet flowers on tall stems.

'Mrs Perry' ht: 1m *3ft* dist: 60cm *2ft*. Salmon pink flowers.

'Perry's White' ht: 90cm *3ft* dist: 60cm *2ft*. Pure-white flowers.

P. rhoeas 'The Shirley' Ann. ht: 30–45cm *12–18in* dist: 23cm *9in* Jun.–Aug. A strain of mixed colours of the field poppy, in shades of red, pink and white, which looks very well amongst other bright-flowered hardy annuals.

The sweetly-scented shrub P. 'Beauclerk'
Mock Orange.

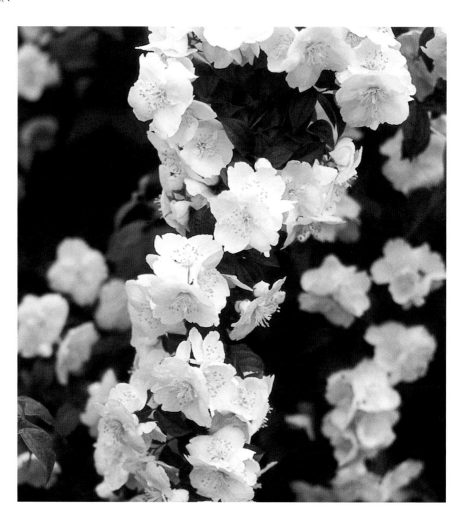

✓   **Philadelphus** (Mock Orange) Nec./Pol. Shr.
Jun.–Jul., full sun, semi-shade.
As an easily grown summer-flowering shrub yielding both nectar and pollen,
the Philadelphus has few equals. The white flowers are produced in profusion
and have the delicious heady fragrance of orange blossom. However, left to
their own devices they tend to become very large plants, up to 4.5m (15ft)
high and as much across. This exuberance can to some extent be controlled
by judicious pruning, but it is far better to choose one of the many excellent
less vigorous cultivars, so that pruning can be kept to an absolute minimum;
remember that all pruning actually reduces the total number of flowers.
The growth habit is intensely twiggy, with new shoots being produced from

the suckering rootstock. The clusters of four-petalled flowers, which may be up to 6cm (2in) in diameter, have a mass of yellow stamens.

'Beauclerk' ht: 2m *6ft* dist: 1.25m *4ft*. This cultivar has the largest flowers, well over 5cm (2in) in diameter.

P. coronarius 'Aureus' ht: 1.25m *4ft* dist: 1m *3ft*. Not as free-flowering as the species, but the golden-green leaves are beautiful. This cultivar needs a sheltered spot, otherwise the leaves will scorch.

P. microphyllus ht: 1m *3ft* dist: 60cm *2ft*. A gem of a plant, with small leaves and strongly scented flowers.

Phlox Pol.

The narrow flower tubes of both the herbaceous and alpine Phlox are too long for nectar (which in any case is only produced in small quantities) to be collected by the honey bee. The colour range in both types is, however, superb and they are commonly seen in most gardens. The alpine types bear their five-petalled flowers in spring or early summer, the herbaceous types in autumn. All have five accessible anthers baring bright yellow pollen.

PHLOX: ALPINE TYPES

The leaves are generally small and lance-shaped, obscured completely by sheets of flower during the relatively short but splendid flowering period.

P. adsurgans ht: 23cm *9in* dist: 30–45cm *12–18in* Jun., acid, semi-shade. Shiny leaves and 2cm (0.75in) shell-pink flowers with a deeper eye.

P. amoena 'Variegata' ht: 12.5cm *5in* dist: 30cm *12in* May–Jun., full sun. Attractively variegated foliage with vivid-pink flowers up to 2.5cm (1in) across.

P. douglasii ht: 12.5cm *5in* dist: 45–60cm *18–24in* May, full sun, semi-shade. Forms large mats of rather straggly foliage, bearing pretty 1.5cm (0.66in) diameter flowers. Blue, white and pink cultivars are commonly available.

P. subulata ht: 12.5cm *5in* dist: 60–90cm *2–3ft* May, full sun. Even more invasive than *douglasii*, but it is easy to forgive such a fabulously free-flowering plant. Just remember to chop back (short back and sides) as soon as the flowering period is over. Cultivars in a wide range of colours are available, the most striking of which is perhaps 'Temiscaming', with its vivid cerise flowers. 'G.F. Wilson' is pale blue, more subtle, and well worth growing.

PHLOX: HERBACEOUS TYPES H ht: 1–1.25m *3–4ft* dist: 60cm *2ft* Aug.–Oct., full sun.

P. paniculata 2.5cm (1in) flowers in dense, rounded, pyramidal clusters above narrow pointed 10cm (4in) leaves. The flowers last longer and fade less if grown in light shade. The colour range is wide – white to red and red-violet, with all the intermediate tints. Fragrant.

'Harlequin' Purple flowers and handsomely yellow variegated foliage.

'White Admiral' White flowers.

'Starfire' Deep glowing red.

Potentilla Nec./Pol.
There are two distinct types of Potentilla: the shrubby types with persistent stems, and the herbaceous ones.
Shrubby Types (Shrubby Cinquefoils) Shr. Deciduous Jun.-Nov. full sun, semi-shade

The exceptionally long flowering season, coupled with the profusion of flowers, most commonly lemon or bright yellow, make the mound-like Potentillas most valuable garden plants. The flowers, carried singly or in clusters, are around 3cm (1.25in) and are quite flat, allowing easy bee access. The five rounded petals overlap and the colour is less intense on the underside. The flower buds, stems and conspicuous dark-brown stipules are distinctly hairy. Leaves are variable in size, smaller than the flowers, with three–five narrow leaflets divided to the base.

A wide range is available – over fifty in fact – but it would be difficult to make a bad choice. No more than three or four will, however, be on offer in the average garden centre.

P. arbuscula 'Beesii' ht: 90cm *3ft* dist: 60cm *2ft*. The branchlets of the *arbuscula* cultivars are typically shaggy in appearance due to the longer stipules, which are very conspicuous. The golden flowers cover the mounded silvery foliage for most of the summer and autumn.

P. fruticosa 'Elizabeth' ht: 90cm *3ft* dist: 60cm *2ft*. Flowers of rich yellow set off to perfection by the very dainty foliage. An excellent plant.

'Goldfinger' ht: 90cm *3ft* dist: 60cm *2ft*. Has perhaps the largest, deepest golden flowers of all the Potentillas, 'Gold-digger' and 'Klondike' have similar flowers but are a shade paler. 'Klondike' also has much more delicate foliage.

Potentilla *fruticosa*

'Katherine Dykes' ht: 1.5m *5ft* dist: 90cm *3ft*. A vigorous and very widely grown cultivar with an abundance of primrose-coloured flowers.

'Longacre' ht: 1m *3ft* dist: 60cm *2ft*. Similar to 'Elizabeth' but rather more dwarf, with darker foliage and more slender branches.

'Mandshurica' ht: 30cm *1ft* dist: 23cm *9in*. A real little charmer, with white flowers on silvery foliage. Ideal for a sunny spot on the rock garden.

'Princess' ht: 1m *3ft* dist: 60cm *2ft*. With its pink to pale-pink flowers, 'Princess' looks rather like a dwarf thornless dog rose. A very pretty plant that justifiably sells extremely well.

'Red Ace' ht: 1m *3ft* dist: 60cm *2ft*. Its bright colour has ensured that it is now widely grown. See it in flower before you decide.

'Tangerine' ht: 1m *3ft* dist: 60cm *2ft*. Although this plant has a reputation for shyness of flowering it is as profuse in my garden as any other cultivar I have seen. The colour is even and deep. Grow it in light shade to help prevent the flowers fading. Flanked on either side by Anchusa and Nepeta with their blue flowers, the contrast looks good and the bees like all three plants.

POTENTILLAS: HERBACEOUS PLANTS

(Cinquefoils) H. Jun.–Oct., dry, full sun, semi-shade.

Pleasant enough border plants but coarser in leaf, flower and form than their shrubby counterparts. The double and semi-double flowered types are not at all attractive to the honey bee and are not mentioned here. The single-flowered cultivars which are 45m (18in) or so in height are good bee plants and are useful for border edging.

P. atrosanguinea 'Gibsons Scarlet' ht: 30–45cm *12–18in* dist: 30cm *12in.* A very old cultivar that has deservedly retained its popularity. The sprays of blood-red flowers have a darker eye, and look well with the dark-green foliage.

P. nepalensis 'Miss Willmott' ht: 30cm *12in* dist: 23–30cm *9–12in.* Similar in form to 'Gibsons Scarlet' but with deep-pink flowers with a red eye.

'Roxana' ht: 30cm *12in* dist: 23–30cm *9–12in.* Flowers two-toned orange and scarlet.

P. anserina (Silverweed) An attractive creeping plant with leaves shaped rather like the wild briar, but soft and silkily hairy, particularly on the undersides, and yellow flowers about 2cm (0.75in) in diameter. Commonly found by roadsides or waste ground, often growing well in damp heavy soils. It can be invasive and there are perhaps not too many gardeners/beekeepers who would wish to introduce it to their carefully maintained gardens!

✓   **Prunus** Nec./Pol.

Japanese flowering cherries are what most people think of whenever Prunus cherries are mentioned, but the genus is far more diverse than this and includes the apricots, peaches, plums (including gages, damsons and bullaces), bird cherries, almonds, laurels (common and Portuguese) and the 'eating cherries'. In cooler climates such as Britain, the fruiting peaches and apricots are really non-starters, but all the others can do very well indeed. Most of the cherries flower early and so provide a valuable early nectar source, provided frost does not damage the flowers and it is mild enough for it to be produced.

For ease of reference I have divided the cherries into six groups.

EVERGREEN LAURELS Shr. Full sun, semi-shade.

P. laurocerasus (Common or Cherry Laurel) ht: 6m *20ft* dist: 4.5m *15ft* Apr., acid. A large wide-spreading shrub with handsome, leathery 15–18cm (6–7in) leaves with conspicuous yellow-green venation, dull pale-green beneath. The plants grow far too large for most gardens, unless grown as a

A honey bee approaches Prunus *laurocerasus* 'Otto Luyken'.

hedge, for which they are very suitable.

If unclipped they flower very freely, the 15cm (6in) 'candles' being very similar to those of *P. padus*, but erect. In addition to the flowers the undersides of the younger leaves have extra-floral nectaries which attract bees right through the summer, and especially at times when nectar is scarce elsewhere.

Many good cultivars are available, and some of the slender flower candles are followed by small red fruits which eventually turn to a dark purple. Less rampant ones are listed below.

'Otto Luyken' ht: 1.25m *4ft* dist: 1.25m *4ft* Apr. Very much smaller and with narrower leaves than the species, but the flower spikes are just about the same size. A long-standing favourite of mine in its own right, but also as a contrast to more showy plants.

'Zabeliana' ht: 1.25m *4ft* dist: 2m *6ft* Apr. Rather less compact than 'Otto Luyken' and also rather more graceful, with its slightly lax branches and longer willow-like leaves.

P. lusitanica (Portuguese Laurel) ht: 4.5m *15ft* dist: 3m *10ft*. A handsome plant with ovate leaves which are considerably smaller and darker green than those of *laurocerasus*. The petioles and young twigs are a deep burgundy and are a distinct and attractive feature. A much slower grower than *laurocerasus*.

The less-vigorous variegated form 'Variegata' is even more handsome, with its leaf margins irregularly splotched with white. Some pink colouration may also be in evidence on young growths, especially during the winter period.

PLUMS T. ht: 3.5m *12ft* Apr., full sun.

These can form very large trees, so try to obtain them on the rootstock 'Pixy' which should limit your tree's height to 3.5m (12ft) or so, and bring them into fruit more quickly than the traditional rootstocks. Alternatively, grow them on a wall as a fan or espalier, especially if shelter from cold winds is likely to be a problem.

Both the varieties described below are self-fertile and require no pollination. Both are also prone to the bacterial disease Silver Leaf, for which there is no control other than cutting back the branches well beyond the infected area; take care to sterilise your secateurs afterwards with household bleach. It is best to seek expert advice before hacking back 'innocent' plants, since the leaves of some cultivars have a naturally silver appearance. Carry out any pruning that is necessary between March and June so that wounds heal quickly.

'Czar' culinary. A cultivar with beautiful blue-purple 'bloom' fruits. If allowed to ripen well it is also a good eater.

'Victoria' The best and most reliable cropping dessert plum in the British climate. The fruits are large, egg-shaped and yellow flushed with deep scarlet.

FRUITING CHERRIES T. ht: 3.5m *12ft* Apr., full sun.

Together with the 'flowering' cherries the fruiting types provide the highest nectar concentration levels of any of the Prunus, with the exception of the laurels. Cherry orchards will provide a considerable honey crop in many seasons. The cherries have extra-floral nectaries in the form of two small lumps on the side of the leaf petiole just below the leaf blade.

'Stella' This is a self-fertile cultivar that produces large dark-red heart-shaped fruits even in the more northerly regions of Britain. Again the rootstock 'Pixy' is the best choice for the average-sized garden. They can be grown as free-standing trees or on a wall as an espalier or fan, which will give a measure of protection and encourage bees to visit the flowers.

The delicate pink-tinged Prunus 'Amanogowa'

FLOWERING CHERRIES T. Apr., full sun.

What an enormous choice there is of these lovely trees that flower so profusely that they look like pink, white or cream clouds against a blue spring sky. Make certain that you are buying single-flowered or semi-double cultivars, since double-flowered ones are more likely to be commonly available.

'Amanogowa' ht: 9m *30ft*. The most upright of the flowering cherries, rather like a Lombardy Poplar but covered with fragrant pale-pink semi-double flowers. Its form makes it ideal for confined spaces. For a really superb combination 'Amanogowa' is sometimes grafted at a height of 1.5–1.8m (5–6ft) on to the glossy stems of *P. serrula* (see below).

'Hisakura' ht: 6m *20ft*. Single, or sometimes semi-double, deep-pink flowers and attractive coppery-red young leaves.

'Shirotae' ht: 6m *20ft*. Flowers white, fragrant, single or semi-double, carried in long drooping clusters. The leaves are distinctly 'toothed'.

'Tai Haku' (Great White Cherry) ht: 10.5m *35ft*. The common name fits this magnificent tree well. There is a group of them at Dartington Hall in Devon, standing close to tall dark-green yew hedges against which they are just breathtaking when in full flower.

They are wide spreading trees 9–12m (30–40ft) and they do cast deep shade, so are not really suitable for any but the largest of gardens. New growth is coppery.

ORNAMENTAL ALMONDS T. Mar., full sun.

Even earlier flowering than the cherries, but most cultivars are not as showy.

P. dulcis 'Alba' ht: 3.5–4.5m *12–15ft.* White single flowers.

'Erecta' ht: 5.5m *18ft* Suitable for small gardens. Pink flowers.

P. x amygdalo-persica 'Pollardii' ht: 6m *20ft.* This is a cross between peach and almond, and it has larger, deeper-pink flowers than any of the other almonds.

OTHER DECIDUOUS CHERRIES T. full sun.

P. avium (Gean, Mazzard or Wild Cherry) ht: 9m *30ft* Mar.–Apr. Certainly one of the showiest of native flowering trees, widely distributed throughout Europe and with smaller, more delicate white flowers than some of its Japanese counterparts. The trees literally 'hum' with bees during flowering. The small dull red fruits are pleasant enough to eat, but hardly provide a feast. The autumn leaf colour is usually good and is complemented by grey-red fissured bark in older trees. There is also a weeping cultivar, 'Pendula'.

P. cerasifera 'Pissardii' (Purple-Leaved Plum) ht: 7.5m *25ft* Mar.–Apr. A small tree with dark-red foliage which turns a deeper purple as it ages. More commonly grown in Britain as a hedging plant, but elsewhere in Europe it is a fairly common street tree, and very showy. Flowers pale pink.

P. hilleri 'Spire' ht: 6m *20ft* Mar.–Apr. Flowers pale pink; good autumn leaf colour. An ideal tree for the average-sized garden.

P. padus (Bird Cherry) ht: 12m *40ft* May–Jun. The small, white almond-scented flowers with yellowish 'eyes' are grouped together in slender drooping 15cm (6in) candles – like small versions of the horse-chestnut and those of the evergreen cherry laurels. The bark is a very dark brown turning black with age. The fruits too are black. Widely distributed throughout most of Europe.

The cultivar 'Waterii' has 20–23cm (8–9in) candles and is well worth growing if you have the space.

P. sargentii ht: 9m *30ft* Mar. As good to look at in autumn, with its lovely leaf colouration of reds and oranges, as it is in spring with its pink flowers and coppery new growth. One of the very best garden trees.

P. serrula ht: 9m *30ft* May. Grown principally for its brilliant shiny red-brown bark, it can nevertheless be free-flowering, but as the flowers are small, white and unremarkable (and partially hidden by the leaves), they often pass largely unnoticed except by the bees.

P. spinosa (Blackthorn or Sloe) ht: 4.5m *15ft* Mar.–May. Very common in hedgerows throughout Europe. The purple-leaved cultivar 'Purpurea' is a fine shrub/tree and is well worth growing. The plant is usually of little use to the honey bee as it flowers in the 'blackthorn winter', but in a warm season the bees will obtain some very useful early pollen. It is doubtful if they ever get much nectar. The bitter blue-black fruits have a white waxy bloom.

P. subhirtella 'Autumnalis' ht: 4.5m *15ft* Nov.–Mar. Some of the small, whitish, semi-double flowers may be present from November to March. The twigs bearing the flowers are rather thin and lax, and the plant needs a dark background to show off the flowers to their best advantage.

P. x yedoensis ht: 9m *30ft* Mar. Very early flowering, with a profusion of pale pink, almond-scented flowers.

Pulmonaria (Lungwort) Pol. H.
ht: 30cm *1ft* dist: 30cm *1ft*
Jan.–May, semi-shade.
Not in the first rank of bee plants, as the nectar, which is freely produced even on cold days in shady situations, is inaccessible at the bottom of the flower tube. The 8mm (0.33in) flowers funnel out above the calyx into five rounded pinky-blue petals, with five stamens alternating with short tufts of hair clustered round the throat of the funnel, guarding access to the tube itself. The hairy leaves are, in some species, heavily spotted with white, and this is an attractive and distinctive feature.

P. angustifolia An unspotted species with bright-blue flowers.

'Munstead Blue' As above, but dwarfer and very slightly later flowering.

P. officinalis This species, which is native to most of Europe, usually but not always has spotted leaves.

P. saccharata A handsome plant with white-spotted leaves and pinky-blue flowers.

'Argentea' A silver-leaved form.

'Pink Dawn' A pink-flowered form.

Prunus *subhirtella*

All Pulmonarias do well on moist soil well supplied with organic matter, and being ground-huggers are less liable to wind damage than taller plants, and manage to attract a few bees if little pollen is available from other sources.

 Pyracantha (Firethorn) Nec./Pol. Shr.
ht: 3–3.5m *10–12ft* dist: 2.5–3m *8–10ft*
May–Jun., salt tol., full sun, semi-shade.
A rather stiff, angular shrub that bears large clusters of hawthorn-like white flowers, followed by even larger clusters of 6mm (0.25in) bright red, yellow or orange fruits which last well on into winter. Although closely related to the Cotoneasters, the Firethorns are to my mind more showy and distinctive, with their gaunt form, dark-green toothed leaves and spiny stems.

Under suitably warm conditions nectar is profusely produced from the masses of flowers that usually cover the firethorns from head to toe in late spring.

All Pyracanthas are very shade-tolerant, and grow successfully even on north- or east-facing walls. Being non-climbers, horizontal wires 30cm (1ft) or more apart will be required to tie in the vigorous upright branches. Choose five or six branches to cover the wall and tie them in as their growth progresses. But back all side shoots to 5–7.5cm (2–3in) immediately after flowering, as this will encourage the 'stumps' to form fruiting spurs for the following year and give clear view of the newly formed fruit clusters.

Allow a space of at least 2.7 x 2.7m (9ft x 9ft) for any Pyracantha grown as a wall shrub. Those grown on a south-facing wall are far more likely to be visited by bees. Unfortunately, like Cotoneasters, Pyracanthas are prone to fireblight. Only buy container-grown plants.

'Orange Charmer' Very free-fruiting, with clusters of small orange fruits.

'Mojave' Large orange-red berries. Said to be more resistant to the depredations of birds and to fireblight.

'Wateri' Less vigorous than many other cultivars, with bright-red fruits.

 Rhododendron Nec. Shr.
Acid, semi-shade.
Few plants, with the possible exception of the rose, have captured the gardening public's imagination more than the Rhododendrons (Rose Tree), with their great showy clusters of flowers and dark-green leathery leaves. Consequently there are literally thousands of species and hybrids to choose from, many of which are far too large for the average garden.

In spite of their popularity they are not ideal garden plants, for an acid soil is always required and the flowering season is relatively short. In addition, Rhododendrons have had a reputation for producing poisonous nectar –

Rhododendron 'Lady Roseberry', one of the most beautiful hybrids

poisonous to both bees and then to humans in the form of the honey made from it. Traditionally, this related to *R. ponticum*, although more recently *R. thomsonii* has been known to kill colonies collecting it. Upon investigation, the poison andromedotoxin was found to be responsible. If one Rhododendron can produce this poison, it is perhaps also produced by others, but there may well be degrees of poisoning depending on the concentration in the nectar.

The honey bee works a range of Rhododendrons, mostly for nectar, and appears unharmed from what I have seen. Whatever poison there may be would be so diluted under normal 'mixed' garden conditions that it is very unlikely to ever be a serious problem. Large estates with heavy concentrations of Rhododendrons may well be a different story, particularly in hot dry summers when the nectar is unusually concentrated.

SPECIES AND THEIR HYBRIDS

R. augustinii ht: 2.5m *8ft* dist: 2m *6ft* Apr.–May. Small-leaved, with beautiful clear-blue flowers. It is a good idea to see the plants in flower before purchasing since there are many inferior purplish-flowered forms in cultivation. Definitely one of the best Rhododendrons for the medium to large garden.

R. campylogynum ht: 30cm *1ft* dist: 60cm *2ft* Apr.–May. Small shiny leaves with deep purplish-brown, waxy, bell-shaped flowers.

R. impeditum ht: 23cm *9in* dist: 45cm *18in* Apr.–May. An ideal plant for the rock garden, with tiny aromatic leaves and bluish-purple, funnel-shaped flowers. Slow grower.

R. scintillans ht: 60cm *2ft* dist: 60cm *2ft* Apr.–May. Small-leaved, with small lavender-blue funnel-shaped flowers.

R. yakushimanum ht:1m *3ft* dist: 1m *3ft* Apr.–May. I first saw this most beautiful of all the larger-flowered dwarf Rhododendrons in the mid-1960s, and was immediately captivated by its dense rounded habit and clusters of rose-pink flower buds which open to the palest apple-blossom pink. It has the form and flower of the larger hybrids without their size. There are a number of cultivars with flowers ranging from white to red.The number of hybrid Rhododendrons available is legion. Choose them with care, particularly with regard to their ultimate size, and remember that a border filled with them will be a pretty sombre spectacle for ten months of the year.

'Blue Diamond' ht: 1m *3ft* dist: 1m *3ft* Apr.–May. Lavender-blue flowers, aromatic foliage.

'Chikor' ht: 45cm *18in* dist: 60cm *2ft* Apr.–May. Small leaves and freely-produced bright yellow flowers.

'Doncaster' ht: 1.25m *4ft* dist: 1.25m *4ft* Apr.–May. Funnel-shaped, crimson-scarlet flowers with black markings inside, and dark-green leaves.

'Jenny' ht: 23cm *9in* dist: 60cm *2ft* Apr.–May. A real ground-hugger, with deep red, bell-shaped flowers. If Rhododendron nectar is poisonous then 'Jenny' should be a killer, for large quantities of nectar are produced at the bases of the deep red bell-shaped flowers. However, the honey bees which eagerly work the flowers appear not to be harmed by it.

'Scarlet Wonder' ht: 60cm *2ft* dist: 60cm *2ft* Apr.–May. Trumpet-shaped flowers with frilly petals.

The hybrids 'Britannia' (crimson-scarlet), 'Cynthia' (rose-crimson), 'Pink Pearl' and 'Purple Splendour' are all ultimately too large for most gardens, but will no doubt continue to be grown, for they are irresistible when in full flower and are commonly available.

AZALEAS

The Azaleas, as they are known (and will no doubt continue to be known by

DECIDUOUS AZALEAS ht: 1.5m *5ft* dist: 1.5m *5ft* May–Jun.

There are several groups to choose from, and a wide range of cultivars in each.

'Gloria Mundi' Bright-orange flowers, an unbelievable sight when in full flower.

'Kosters Brilliant Red' A deservedly very popular cultivar.

'Cecile' Deep pink, becoming paler as it opens, with yellow in the flared throat.

'Lemonora' Deep apricot-yellow, with a red tinge on the outside.

'Satan' Blood-red flowers with a trace of yellow staining at the base of the petals.

EVERGREEN AZALEAS ht: 1m *3ft* dist: 1–1.25m *3–4ft* Apr–May.

There are a large number of groups of evergreens and a bewildering choice of cultivars and colours, all of which flower profusely.

'Addy Werry' Deep vermilion red.

'Blaauws Pink' Salmon-pink with paler shading.

'Hinodegiri' Bright crimson.

'Orange Beauty' Salmon-orange.

'Palestrina' A real cracker, with crows of white flowers with the palest of apple-green eyes. If you have space for just one cultivar, then make it this one.

'Vuyks Scarlet' Bright red with frilled petals.

everyone except the botanists) are also classified as Rhododendrons. These are more suitable for the average to small garden, since they are usually in scale with it, averaging around 90–150cm (3–5ft) in height. There are both deciduous and evergreen types.

Ribes Nec./Pol. Shr.   ✓
Full sun, semi-shade.

This undemanding, large and varied genus contains the common (but nonetheless showy) flowering currants, together with their fruiting counterparts, the black, white and red currants and gooseberries, all of which (with the exception of blackcurrants) can be grown as cordons if space is limited. In areas where these fruits are grown on a large commercial scale (blackcurrants in particular), they can provide extensive bee forage areas.

The leaves are usually palmate and, together with the stems, often emit a distinct 'currant' odour. The individual flowers are small and somewhat tubular, but the numbers on each pendulous cluster are so large that when they are brightly coloured they make a considerable impact.

ORNAMENTAL TYPES

R. odoratum ht: 2m *6ft* dist: 1.5m *5ft* Mar.–Apr. Often sold as *aureum* which, if not botanically accurate, sounds more pleasant. The odour in this case is a very pleasant one indeed, and if you have the space this golden-flowered currant is well worth having. The leaves are a shining green changing to gold in the autumn, and the black berries are particularly showy.

R. sanguineum ht: 2.75m *9ft* dist: 2–2.25m *6–7ft* Mar.–Apr. The cultivars of this species are known as the flowering currants, and are available in a range of colours from white through the pinks to deep red. All have the distinctive musky current smell. The black berries, unlike those of *odoratum* are not a very distinctive feature.

'Albescens' Flowers white with pink tinge.

'Brocklebankii' Golden-yellow leaves with pink flowers, rather less vigorous than the green-leaved forms.

'King Edward VII' Crimson flowers, rather less vigorous than the type.

'Pulborough Scarlet' Large deep-crimson flowers, well worth seeking out over and above any of the other listed cultivars.

R. speciosum (Fuchsia-Flowered Currant) ht: 2.25–2.5m *7–9ft* dist: 2m *6ft* May. With its spiny stems and shiny leaves, this distinctive species is a superb sight when the branches are laden with rows of the short, pendulous, crimson flowers, from which protrude conspicuous red stamens. It comes into leaf in winter, long before it is sensible to do so, and as a consequence frequently suffers frost damage. Packing it in among other shrubs seems to give sufficient protection.

FRUITING TYPES

ht: 1.25–1.5m *4–5ft* dist: 1.25–1.5m *4–5ft* Apr.–May. These are also well known as to make detailed descriptions unnecessary. Some recommended cultivars are listed below.

BLACKCURRANTS

'Blackdown' Fairly early flowering, resistant to mildew.

'Jet' Flowers later than most other cultivars, and therefore usually escapes frost damage.

'Ben Lomond' also flowers later and is resistant to mildew.

REDCURRANTS AND WHITECURRANTS

Protect the fruit of red and white currants against birds. Both may be grown as single or double cordons if space is limited, so buy them ready trained. Redcurrants are vigorous and will grow to 2–2.5m (7–8ft) if left unchecked. Recommended are 'Red Lane', 'Stanza' (late flowering), and 'White Versailles'.

GOOSEBERRIES

These are unfortunately normally picked when immature – hard, green, flavourless. After the bees have taken their fill of pollen and nectar from the flowers, leave the fruits to hang until August and September (true for most cultivars). You will know when they are really ripe by their colour and by giving them the 'squeeze test'. They may be well over 3.5cm (1.5in) in diameter at this stage, and deliciously sweet and juicy. Recommended are 'Careless', pale greeny-white when ripe; 'Leveller', yellow when ripe; and 'Whinhams Industry', red when ripe.

Gooseberries may also be grown as cordons 30–45cm (12–18in) apart from where space is limited. As with all other fruit, correct and regular pruning is required if maximum crops are to be obtained.

R. coulteri. The number of bees on this flower is evidence of its popularity

Romneya coulteri (Californian or Tree Poppy) Nec./Pol. Shr.
ht: 1.5–2m *5–6ft* dist: 1–1.25m *3–4ft*
Jul.–Oct., full sun.
The six-petalled flowers, white and fragrant, can be up to 15cm (6in) in diameter and have as their centrepiece a large golden boss of stamens to which bees flock in great numbers. The overlapping petals have a satiny texture, and appear very flimsy in relation to their relatively large size, as they move easily in the slightest breeze.

The leaves are thick, 16cm (6in) or so long, glaucous and deeply cut, rather like a hand with the central 'finger' longest. Romneya is classified as a shrub, but is similar to a herbaceous plant, since the thick-green stems are often killed back to the suckering rootstock in severe winters, from which new shoots are produced again in spring. The fleshy rootstocks are sensitive to disturbance, so try to buy pot-grown plants and thereafter move them only if it is really essential.

Any other species or cultivar would be just as suitable.

Rosa Pol. Shr.
Full sun.
Everybody, or almost everybody, loves roses. If you doubt this, reflect on the fact that around 35 million are sold annually in Britain alone. With the average life of a rose at about ten years it will come as no surprise that nearly every garden in the country boasts at least a few plants.

The colour range, particularly of the smaller more commonly grown garden types, is truly enormous, with single colours, bi-colours, multi-colours, blends, stripes and the so-called hand-painted types. Add to this (in many cases) a delightful fragrance, long flowering season, with no long wait for the first flowers after planting and ease of culture; the rose provides what is required from a good garden plant. Many of the more commonly grown types – hybrid tea (now more correctly called 'large-flowered'), and to a lesser extent floribundas (now called 'cluster-flowered') – are largely unsuitable for the bee friendly garden, since the flowers are mostly double or at best semi-double. For this reason hybrid tea roses will not be covered here.

The shrub roses are classified separately and they really are a mixture of old, nineteenth-century and new types. They are frequently taller and more robust than the types mentioned above, and often have a shorter flowering season. But, they compensate for this with literally masses of flowers – single in many species and cultivars – which open to reveal a central boss packed with golden stamens. The fragrant flowers alone are attraction enough, but add to this a variety of other attributes, the attractive foliage and fruit and even great 'winged' translucent red thorns, and you have one of the most versatile and beautiful of all plants.

Climbers, and to a lesser extent ramblers, are also very popular, and the dwarf miniatures continue to increase in popularity. There are single-flowered species and cultivars of each of these types.

Do not forget to remove the old flowers when they are 'blown' and the stamens are brown. Failure to do so may well prevent more flowers from being produced. With only pollen on offer at a time of year when there is plenty else available, roses will never be a beekeeper's first choice, but few will find this a reason for not growing at least some.

If you see a rose you like that is not described here, then check its credentials in any good book on roses, and if it meets your requirements, buy it.

FLORIBUNDAS (Cluster-Flowered) Jun.–Sep.

Those cultivars with the fewest petals are a good choice – the singles and semi-doubles.

'Anna Wheatcroft' ht: 1m *3ft* dist: 45–60cm *18–24in*. Large flat semi-double flowers of light vermilion. Slightly fragrant.

'Escapade' ht: 1m *3ft* dist: 45–60cm *18–24in*. A most attractive rose with large flat blooms. The lilac petals are white towards the centre. Musk-like fragrance.

'Dainty Maid' ht: 1m *3ft* dist: 45–60cm *18–24in*. Silvery pink petals with a carmine reverse, slightly fragrant.

'Eye Paint' ht: 1.5m *5ft* dist: 1–1.25m *3–4ft*. Although the flowers are somewhat small, their colouring (scarlet with a white eye) and number more than compensate, and make this a real 'impact' plant.

'Fervid' ht: 1m *3ft* dist: 60cm *2ft*. Vivid scarlet, slightly fragrant flowers that retain their colour well.

'Masquerade' ht: 1m *3ft* dist: 45–60cm *18–24in*. This was the first multi-coloured cultivar to be produced. All the colour variations occur at the same time on the large flower trusses, yellow, pink and eventually dark red. It is free-flowering and slightly scented. Well worth a place in the garden, and just as good in its diminutive form (Baby Masquerade) or its climbing form, see 'Climbers' section below.

'Paprika' ht: 75cm *2.5ft* dist: 45cm *18in*. The flowers are bright geranium red with a bluish tinge towards the base of the petals. Vigorous and easy to grow. The flowers do not suffer weather damage to the same degree as some other cultivars.

MINIATURES Jun.–Sep.

As the name suggests, these roses are considerably smaller than either the hybrid teas or floribundas. For the smallest garden, as an edging.

There are no single cultivars and few worthwhile semi-doubles.

'Josephine Wheatcroft' ht: 39cm *15in* dist: 30cm *12in*. Bright-yellow flowers.

'Perla De Montserrat' ht: 23cm *9in* dist: 15–23cm *6–9in*. Clear-pink flowers, paler at the edges.

'Starina' ht: 45cm *18in* dist: 30m *12in*. Orange-red flowers, vigorous.

SHRUB ROSES

The flowers and growth habits of these most diverse plants are as beautiful and varied as some of the group names would suggest – Musk, Bourbon, China, Gallica, Damask, Moss, Centifolia. You should not, however, be swayed by just a name. Make certain that the cultivar, species or variety you have seen in a garden, catalogue or book meets your requirements, particularly with regard to size (many of them are too large for the average garden and they do not respond well to the severe pruning meted out to hybrid teas and floribundas) and flowering period (flowering periods are frequently short). Single or semi-double flowers are also essential if the bees are to derive any benefit. For reference, the group or type to which each rose belongs is shown in brackets after its name.

'Angelina' (Modern Shrub) ht: 105cm *3.5ft* dist: 75–90cm *2.5–3ft* Jul.–Oct. Pretty deep-pink semi-double flowers with a white edge. Slightly fragrant.

'Balerina' (Modern Shrub) ht: 1.25m *4ft* dist: 1m *3ft* Jul.–Oct. Masses of single pink flowers with a large white edge are produced right through the summer and autumn. Slight musk fragrance. The small glossy leaves are attractive and complementary to the flowers.

'Berlin' (Modern Shrub) ht: 1.5m *5ft* dist: 1.25m *4ft* Jul.–Oct. Large single orange-scarlet flowers produced intermittently over a long season. Slightly scented. Foliage dark and leathery, thorns large and red.

'Canary Bird' (Species) ht: 2.25m *7ft* dist: 1.5–2m *5–6ft* May–Jun. A very early and profuse flowerer, but it will not provide pollen for bees for more than a few weeks. The flowers are bright yellow, single and about 5cm (2in) across. The foliage is grey-green and delicate with small leaflets.

'Frau Dagmar Hartopp' (Rugosa) ht: 1.5m *5ft* dist: 1.25m *4ft* Jul.–Oct. Beautiful shell-pink flowers, 9cm (3in) across, which are perfectly complemented by the dark Rugosa-type foliage. Superb large bright-red hips and good autumn leaf colour.

'Max Graf' (Rugosa) ht: 30cm *1ft* dist: 1.25m *4ft* Jul.–Aug. Again the typical Rugosa foliage, carried on prostrate stems. Single pink fragrant flowers with a white centre. Unfortunately the flowering season is rather short. Good ground-cover plant.

'Nozomi' (Modern Shrub) ht: 60cm *2ft* dist: 1.25m *4ft* Jul.–Aug. A neater but more sparse ground-cover plant than the preceding cultivar. The small pink flowers are carried in clusters and have no fragrance. Short flowering season. The foliage is dark green.

R. rubrifolia syn. *ferruginea* (Species) ht: 2.25m *7ft* dist: 1.5–2m *5–6ft* Jul.–Aug. Flowers small, usually less than 5cm (2in) in diameter, pale pink with a white eye. Combined with handsome blue-grey foliage, this makes a fine plant for the mixed border. Bright-red hips as early as August and September are a further bonus.

'Yesterday' ht: 1m *3ft* dist: 45–60cm *18–24in* Jul.–Oct. Profuse, dainty, scented semi-double flowers, mauve-pink with a silver edge.

CLIMBERS Jun.–Sep.

Few private gardens have the space or the budget for the traditional rose pergola; most gardens will only find space for one or two climbers, grown up a single pole, wigwam or on a wall.

'Altissimo' ht: 2.5m *8ft.* Single 12.5cm (5in) blood-red slightly fragrant flowers that first appear in June.

'Dortmund' ht: 2.25m *7ft.* Large single crimson flowers with a white edge, freely carried. No noticeable fragrance. Can, by severe pruning, be kept as a large 'shrub'.

'Masquerade' ht: 2.5m *8ft.* The climbing form of the floribunda with its multi-coloured flower trusses. This rose in full flower viewed against a blue sky is a spectacular sight.

'Meg' ht: 3.5m *12ft.* Salmon-apricot, semi-double flowers 12.5cm (5in) in diameter, with a large central boss of red-orange stamens. Fragrant.

Rosmarinus officinalis (Rosemary) Nec./Pol. Shr.
ht: 1–1.25m *3–4ft* dist: 60–90cm *2–3ft*
Apr.–Jun., dry, salt tol., full sun.
One of the constituents of the maquis, the dense and strongly aromatic collection of plants found particularly in Corsica, but also in other Mediterranean regions. The hotter it becomes the stronger the aroma but, above all, the distinctive aroma of rosemary can be enjoyed. It is a veritable weed in these areas but is an important bee plant, and bees are invariably seen clustering on its pale-blue flowers. The two-lipped flowers are grouped in the leaf axils along the branches on the previous season's growth.

R. officinalis, Rosemary

The slender, erect branches are thickly clothed with short, narrow unstalked leaves, glossy green above with inrolled margins partly obscuring the grey undersides.

Hard and long periods of frost may kill parts of your plants and will almost certainly prevent them from reaching their full potential of 2m (6ft) in height. Rosemary is, however, a fast growing plant, so replacement should not be too much of a problem, especially if some cuttings are taken each year in August as an insurance against possible winter losses.

Only relatively hardy cultivars have been included here.

'Albus' White flowers.

'Majorca' Bright blue with a darker spot on the bottom flower lip.

'Miss Jessup's Variety' syn. 'Fastigiatus' A very erect form.

'Roseus' Lilac-pink flowers and somewhat less vigorous than the type.

'Severn Sea' Bright-blue flowers, less upright with more arching branches.

✓ **Rubus** Nec./Pol. Shr.
Many of the plants in this genus are not only attractive to bees, they also bear edible fruits: blackberry, raspberry and loganberry (and the newer hybrids thereof). This group will be dealt with separately from the ornamental types, some of which are quite outstandingly decorative garden plants and attract bees in numbers commensurate with the large numbers of stamens.

BLACKBERRY or BRAMBLE Shr. ht: 3m *10ft* dist: 3.5–4.5m *12–15ft* Jul.–Oct., full sun, semi-shade.
This must be one of the most undisciplined of plants, with its long lax stems flopping in all directions and its tips rooting into the ground where they touch. It is, however, a major source of pollen and nectar (from the wild), when few others are available.

The blackberry's sprawling habit is best 'restrained' and trained in some way. If you have a post and wire fence then this will do reasonably well as a support – provided there is at least a clear 4.5m (15ft) run! Ideally the support should be 2m (6ft) high with horizontal wires every 30cm (12in) for tying in. Train and tie all of one year's canes to one side and all the next year's to the other.

There are good cultivars grown commercially both with and without thorns. The white or variably pink flowers are carried in clusters, and are an attractive feature. The delicious shiny black fruits are too well known to need describing in detail and the leaflets, of which there are five–seven, are strongly serrated, dark green and similar in general appearance to those of the dog rose.

'Fantasia' Very large fruits. Both 'Oregon Thornless' (Thornless Evergreen) and 'Smoothstem' are thornless, and may well appeal to the gardener who does not want to get bloodied when picking the fruit, a not infrequent occurrence with some of the older thorny cultivars such as 'Bedford Giant' and 'Himalayan Giant'.

RASPBERRY ht: 2–2.25m *6–7ft* dist: 30–45cm *12–18in* full sun, semi-shade.

In areas where raspberries are widely grown (such as Tayside and Fife in north-east Scotland) the honey that is produced is highly prized and is regarded as perhaps the finest available. Bees are attracted in great numbers, even when dull conditions prevail, possibly because the sugar concentration in the nectar is very high. Flowering somewhat later than many other fruits the flowers, which are carried on short side shoots, are rarely damaged by frost; their pendulous habit also helps to prevent the nectar from being diluted by rain. As with oil-seed rape, however, the honey granulates quickly and needs to be removed early. The canes are usually supported by a post and wire fence, the numerous suckering shoots being tied in at a 7.5cm (3in) spacing.

'Malling Admiral' May–Jun. A good all-round cultivar with a long flowering and fruiting season.

'Malling Autumn Bliss' Jul.–Oct. One of the newer and better autumn flowering/fruiting cultivars.

LOGANBERRY ht: 3m *10ft* dist: 3.5–4.5m *12–15ft* May–Jun., full sun.

The fruits of the loganberry are a much darker red than those of the raspberry and also much longer. The cloned LY654, usually simply called Thornless Loganberry, is widely available.

ORNAMENTAL TYPES

R. cockburnianus ht: 2.5m *8ft* dist: 1.5–2m *5–6ft* May–Jun., full sun, semi-shade. The gently arching thorny purple stems are heavily overlaid with a white bloom, making this a most striking plant during the long winter months. The leaves are grey-white, the small but plentiful flowers are followed by black fruits.

R. x tridel 'Benenden' ht: 3m *10ft* dist: 2.5–3m *8–10ft* May–Jun., full sun. A most beautiful and graceful shrub whose masses of pure white flowers, with their centre literally packed with golden stamens, are irresistible to bees. The flowers can be up to 7.5cm (3in) across and yield prodigious amounts of pollen. If you have the space, then this non-thorny cultivar is a must.

Salix (Willow or Sallow) Nec./Pol.
Full sun, semi-shade.
This is an enormously variable genus, including some giants, but also a good number of wild species (and perhaps an even larger number of hybrids arising from them). It is still well worth planting at least one species or cultivar in every garden, for they are a rich source of early pollen (the more showy male forms only), and it is wonderful to see the bees working the pollen-covered catkins in the early spring.

Both male and female plants yield nectar from yellowish glands at the base of the stamens or pistil, and these can clearly be seen if a large catkin of, say, *S. lanata*, is broken open. Try to make absolutely certain that the plants you buy are males, for as well as bearing no pollen the females flower far too early to be at all reliable as a nectar source.

Keep the larger tree willows well away from buildings and avoid the very tempting golden weeping willow (*S. x chrysocoma*), unless you have plenty of space and are prepared to spray it regularly for canker and scab: quite disfiguring diseases to which this hybrid is particularly susceptible. Spraying a small tree is easy, a large one is almost impossible.

Several of the willows, such as *alba* 'Britzensis' and *daphnoides*, are grown principally for their winter stem colouration, but for this to be retained they need to be cut down annually in spring. This means they look good over winter, but bear no catkins, so are of no use to bees when so treated.

Male catkins of *S. caprea* with honey bee

S. aegyptica Shr/T. ht: 5.5m *18ft* dist: 5.5m *18ft* Feb.–Mar. Large bright-yellow catkins and lance-shaped leaves carried on softly hairy grey twigs. Very showy.

S. caprea (Palm or Goat Willow) Shr./T. ht: 6–9m *20–30ft* dist: 6–9m *20–30ft* Feb.–Mar. Usually seen as a large shrub or small tree and most conspicuous in the early spring when covered with the 2.5cm (1in) ovoid male catkins, rather like grey power-puffs. These are crowded together at the ends of the branches and as the stamens emerge they turn a beautiful golden yellow. The female form is known as Pussy Willow and has longer, narrower grey catkins. A real favourite with bees and beekeepers alike, and if you have the space, the Goat Willow is a must.

'Pendula' T. ht: 2.25m *7ft* dist: 2–2.25m *6–7ft* Mar.–Apr. This graceful weeping tree, very suitable for a small garden, is a delight, particularly during the winter and spring. As the leaves turn bright yellow and fall in the autumn, the small silver catkins protrude from the copper-coloured buds to provide bright silver dots down the trailing branches during the winter. In the spring the catkins increase in size, and at flowering time are the large fluffy yellow balls, covered in pollen, so beloved by the honey bee. This applies only to a male tree, which may be rather difficult to come by, but if you look around the garden centres in March the trees in containers should be in flower and a male can be selected.

S. hastate 'Wehrhanii' Shr. ht: 1.25m *4ft* dist: 1.25m *4ft* Feb.–Mar. An ideal willow for the smaller garden. The reddish-brown twigs are crowded with silvery-white catkins which later turn yellow.

S. lanata (Woolly Willow) Shr. ht: 1.25m *4ft* dist: 1.25–1.5m *4–5ft* May–Jul. All too rare in most gardens, for it is a superb plant and in mid-winter provides interest with its fat swollen woolly buds, persistent stipules and yellow stems. The male catkins are yellow and somewhat ovoid, up to 5cm (2in) long. Catkins of the female form may, however, lengthen considerably – up to 10m (4in) – in fruit. The leaves are broad and handsome, almost circular, silvery grey and downy, turning a beautiful yellow in autumn. Certainly a more interesting plant than *caprea* and an ideal substitute for it in the smaller garden.

S. melanostachys syn. *gracilistyla* Shr. ht: 2m *6ft* dist: 2m *6ft* May–Jun. This species has very distinctive catkins, the bud scales of which are black, opening to reveal brick-red anthers which turn yellow as they age. The grey-green leaves are 10cm (4in) in length.

S. reticulata Shr. ht: 15cm *6in* dist: 30–38cm *12–15in* May–Jun. Another rare willow, this time of diminutive form, which lives up to its name by having conspicuous net venation on its shiny roundish leaves. The erect catkins appear after the leaves. Well worth growing and ideal for the rock garden.

Many of the other willows will form very large plants indeed, so take great care before making a purchase, however attractive they appear. Two cultivars in this category very commonly seen in garden centres are the twisted-stem *matsudana* 'Tortuosa' (which is only available in its female form), and *sachalinensis* 'Sekka', with its flattened and recurved stems.

None of the species listed needs a wet soil, and most are in fact very tolerant of dry conditions.

Salvia Nec./Pol.
Full sun.
The scarlet Salvias used for summer bedding schemes are not suitable for honey bees, since the two-lipped flower tube is far too long for them to reach the nectar. Fortunately there are many other Salvias which do not have this disadvantage and are far more useful and decorative, and in some cases can be guaranteed to be covered in honey bees from the time the first flowers appear.

S. farinacea Ann. ht: 38cm *15in* dist: 30cm *12in* Jun.–Nov. A fine annual bedding plant. The flower spikes bear masses of small violet-blue flowers encased in woolly white calyces. Far too decorative a plant to keep just for annual bedding schemes; use them also for herbaceous and shrub borders.

S. viridis syn. *horminum* (Clary) A(h). ht: 45cm *18in* dist: 15–23cm *6–9in* May–Oct. The small lilac-coloured flowers of this species are insignificant, hidden as they are by the large variously coloured bracts – pink, white, blue, and purple, with darker venation. The bracts retain their colour when dry and are very useful for winter decorations.

S. officinalis (Sage) Shr. ht: 60cm *2ft* dist: 60–90cm *2–3ft* May–Jul. A strongly aromatic shrub with thick grey-green wrinkled leaves and violet-blue flowers carried in loose whorls. The purple form 'Purpurescens' has darker flowers and the occasional variegated shoot, with splashes of pink, cream and purple. The golden sage 'Icterina' is particularly colourful, with its delightful marbled pale green, gold and lemon leaves. I have never seen it flower, but it may well do so in a drier, sunnier spot than where mine is located. I have all three forms in my garden and can never decide which one I like the best. They are all equally good for flavouring, and all three suffer in severe winters, for which reason I leave any pruning that is to be done until March so the tips of the shoots, even if they are dead, help to protect those lower down. Fortunately, cuttings taken any time between June and September root like weeds. A dry soil is desirable but not essential.

S. x superba H. ht: 60cm *2ft* dist: 45cm *18in* Jun.–Sep. Stiff spikes of intense purple-blue flowers with crimson bracts, set against grey-green leaves. The cultivar 'Lubeca' has deeper blue flowers, and both have persistent rusty brown dead flower heads and bracts, making an attractive end-of-season display.

Use these spikey plants in any border to help break up the mounded effect of the plant forms that can dominate gardens. Good bee and colour combinations would be *S. x superba* planted with grey foliage plants such as Stachys *lanata*, Senecio 'Sunshine' or Salix *lanata*.

Saxifraga (Rock Foil) Nec./Pol.
Translated, Saxifraga literally means rock-breaker, an allusion to the effect that some of the species, particularly those that grow in rock crevices, will in time have on their 'homes'. The Saxifrages are one of the darlings of the alpine plant enthusiasts, and understandably so, for whether they form carpets or tight mounded hummocks there are few other alpines that flower so freely and in such a wide colour range. Unfortunately, the flowers are not especially popular with the bees, in spite of nectar being freely available. The flowers, with 4–5 rounded petals, are usually carried on branched stems which bear scale-like leaves. The true leaves can be very variable and in some species may be parsley-like, or toothed and paddle-shaped, or – showiest of all – linear and toothed with white encrustations of lime along their edge.

The choice is truly enormous, so I have limited here to a few favourites; try one or two and if your bees do make good use of them, plant some more!

S. x elizabethae ht: 12.5cm *5in* dist: 30cm *12in* Mar.–Apr., full sun, semi-shade. Yellow flowers very freely produced on rapidly spreading mats of foliage. Planted with *x jenkinsae*, which has silvery foliage and pale-pink flowers, there can be few more pleasing plant combinations. Plant both amongst rocks rather than 'on' them.

S. oppositifolia ht: 2.5cm *1in* dist: 23cm *9in* Mar.–Apr., full sun. The very best of all the Saxifrages, with its bright-pink ground-hugging flowers and bright orange-tipped stamens. The tiny rounded leaves are packed together and are completely obscured by the flowers. So striking is this plant when seen in a colourless windswept mountain setting it is difficult to believe that anything so beautiful and seemingly delicate could exist in such a place. Grows most happily in rock crevices throughout much of Europe.

S. paniculata syn. *aizoon* ht: 23–30cm *9–12in* dist: 23–30cm *9–12in* May–Jun., full sun, semi-shade. Forms dense tight hummocks of grey-green rosettes, 30cm (12in) or so across. The rosettes are on short rooting stems, by which means it spreads itself. The leaves can be up to 5cm (2in) long, slightly upturned at the ends, and with conspicuous saw-like teeth, all encrusted with limey deposits. The bases of all the leaves have conspicuous burgundy-red colouration.

The flower clusters are rather loose and the individual flowers rather small, usually white or pale cream in colour, although there are yellow and pink forms also. Very easily grown in rock crevices or in soil.

S. x urbium syn. *umbrosa* (London Pride) ht: 30cm *12in* dist: 20–23cm *8–9in* May–Jun., semi-shade. The cultivar 'Elliot's Variety', as 23–25cm (9–10in) is more dwarf than the type and carries masses of small star-like pink flowers.

'Mossy Saxifrages' ht: 10–23cm *4–9in* dist: 23–30cm *9–12in* Apr.–May, semi-shade. The hybrid mossy Saxifrages, so called because their mat-like foliage resembles moss, are perhaps the easiest to grow of all the Saxifrages, and there are a large number of cultivars. 'Bob Hawkins' has variegated foliage and white flowers, 'Red Admiral' has, as its name suggests, bright-red flowers. All the cultivars are showy and well worth growing.

The majority of the Saxifrages prefer limey soils and are best planted in rock gardens or scree beds in association with other alpines.

Scabiosa Nec./Pol. H.
Jun.–Oct., full sun.
The wild blue Scabious and its close relatives – visually and botanically – Knautia (Field Scabious) and Succisa (Devil's Bit Scabious), are found in abundance in hedgerows on dry banks, particularly on chalky soil, throughout

most of Europe. All are equally attractive to bees and between them provide nectar from June to October.

The outer florets of the flowers are generally much larger and appear like the petals of a normal flower. Each tubular-shaped floret has four–five lobes, is 6mm (0.25in) or so long, and surrounded by dark-brown sepals and a funnel-shaped structure with a 'grass skirt' attached to it, which partially covers the sepals. The long stamens protruding from the smaller inner florets earn the scabious one of its common names, the Pincushion Flower. All the Scabious make good cut flowers.

S. atropurpurea (Sweet Scabious) ht: 60cm *2ft* dist: 23cm *9in*. Comes in a range of colours from lilac to purple, the flowers being 5cm (2in) in diameter and fragrant. Although it is a short-lived perennial, *atropurpurea* is normally treated as a hardy annual.

S. caucasica ht: 1m *3ft* dist: 60cm *2ft*. It is from this species that the best known garden cultivars have been derived, 'Bressingham White' and 'Clive Greaves' with flowers of a rich lavender-blue with a paler centre. This last cultivar has been popular for many years. There are newer dwarfer cultivars such as 'Butterfly Blue'.

'Moerheim Beauty' Deeper blue than 'Clive Greaves'.

S. graminifolia ht: 23cm *9in* dist: 15–23cm *6–9in*. Flowers mauve-blue, with silvery foliage.

'Pinkushion' Pink flowers and silvery foliage.

Scilla Nec./Pol. B./C.
Full sun, semi-shade.
Easily grown, showy bulbous plants related to the hyacinths and grape hyacinths, mostly with blue nodding flowers that vary in shape from bell (as in the bluebell) to shallow dish (as in the vibrant *S. sibirica)*. The flowers are in fact 'tepals', the petals and sepals being fused. The leaves are all basal, and long and narrow, sometimes barely appearing before the flowers.

Although they will not tolerate the dense shade beneath evergreens, they do well enough beneath deciduous trees and close to deciduous shrubs, as long as it is not too dry. If they are happy you will soon know, for all the Scillas seed themselves freely under such conditions. Plant the bulbs about 5cm (2in) deep.

S. bifolia ht: 10cm *4in* dist: 10cm *4in* Mar.–Apr. Flat star-shaped flowers, also available in white and pink forms.

S. non-scripta syn. *Endymion non-scriptus* syn. *Hyacinthoides non-scripta* ht: 30cm *12in* dist: 10–15cm *4–6in* Apr.–Jun. The common bluebell is a vigorous plant that will soon smother plants of a less robust nature, so choose its companions with care. They are best located in a deciduous woodland setting where they look perfect and can colonise to their hearts' content. The small nodding flowers, of which there are several per stem, are truly bell-shaped and effectively prevent direct entry by the honey bee to the nectar. The six tepals are, however, divided to the base and it is not too difficult for the honey bee to gain access to the nectar via this route. At times when nectar is freely produced, it is also exuded between the tepals.

Pink and white forms are not uncommon in the wild, and are usually available commercially.

S. sibirica ht: 12.5cm *5in* dist: 7.5–10cm *3–4in* Mar.–Apr. Deep gentian-blue, slightly cupped flowers, carried very freely, make this one of the most popular early spring-flowering bulbs. Ideal for the rock garden or naturalised in grass, it looks very well when planted in company with dwarf *Narcissus* (such as 'Tete a Tete' or *bulbocodium*), or with primroses.

S. verna ht: 15cm *6in* dist: 10cm *4in* Mar.–Jun. A pretty pale-blue-flowered plant, very suitable for the rock garden or naturalised in short grass. The flowers, which are relatively large – up to 16mm (0.66in) in diameter – are carried in terminal clusters of between two and twelve.

Sedum Nec.
Full sun.
Few gardeners would want to manage without at least one of these easily grown

S. spectabile just coming into flower, with bees already raiding its nectar plants. The individual flowers are small in size (similar to Saxifrages) but large in number, literally hundreds of them being carried in flat heads in many of the species. The leaves are frequently large and with few exceptions succulent, varying in shape from flat to cylindrical.

For convenience I have divided them into two groups; those suitable for rock gardens, and those for herbaceous or even shrub borders.

ROCK GARDEN TYPES H. dry

All the alpine-type species lend themselves well to hot, dry situations such as paths, drystone walls and raised beds.

S. acre (Stonecrop) ht: 7.5cm *3in* dist: 30cm *12in* Jun.–Jul. Many plants that are easy to grow tend to be despised and categorised as 'weeds'. Indeed stonecrop is easy to grow and weed-like in its tendency to invade any piece of bare ground. The soil in my own garden is a rather light sandy loam and it positively revels in these conditions, filling any piece of bare ground (including gravel paths) that presents itself. It also managed to establish itself in a much 'manicured' vegetable garden, and refuses to shrivel and die when pulled out and left on the surface like any normal weed should. It has clusters of vibrant, yellow, star-like flowers, and the bees love it.

S. spathulifolium ht: 7.5cm *3in* dist: 30cm *12in* Jun.–Jul. A compact plant that does spread but could not be described as invasive. The rosettes of spoon-shaped fleshy leaves are covered with a waxy grey bloom. The flower stems and older leaves are often bright red, and the yellow flowers are very similar to those of *acre*.

'Cappa Blanca' ht: 7.5cm *3in* dist: 30cm *12in* Jun.–Jul. The leaf rosettes are silver-grey in winter, turning blue-grey in summer. Yellow flowers.

S. spurium 'Erdblut' ht: 15cm *6in* dist: 45cm *18in* Jun.–Aug. Carmine flowers in dense heads.

'Schorbusser Blut' ht: 15cm *6in* dist: 45cm *18in* Jun.–Aug. Red flowers.

HERBACEOUS OR SHRUB BORDER TYPES H.

S. maximum 'Atropurpureum' ht: 45cm *18in* dist: 45cm *18in* Aug.–Sep. The thick fleshy leaves and stems are purplish-brown and provide interest from spring to autumn. The rose-pink flowers appear in the autumn and contrast well with the foliage.

S. rosea (Rose Root) ht: 30cm *12in* dist: 30cm *12in* May–Jun. The leaves are blue-grey and so closely packed that the stem supporting them is hidden. The lime-green flower heads are small and the leaves can be seen sticking out like a ruff when viewed from above. A striking plant for the spring garden.

S. spectabile ht: 45cm *18in* dist: 45cm *18in* Sep.–Nov. There are many cultivars of this splendid, stiffly erect plant, with its great flat flower heads up to 20–23cm (8–9in) in diameter, which contain many hundreds of individual flowers. Most of the colouration comes from the four or five hollow inflated pistils, which look rather like a crown (as they do in most other Sedum species), and all types of bees and butterflies (peacock butterflies in my own garden) can frequently be seen, probing for nectar. There are no petals as such. A quite beautiful flower when observed closely. The fleshy leaves are over 7.5cm (3in) long, grey-green and saw-toothed in the upper two thirds.

'Autumn Joy' ht: 60cm *2ft* dist: 60cm *2ft.* Flowers rose-red at first, turning to russet in November.

'Brilliant' ht: 45cm *18in* dist: 45cm *18in.* Bright rose-pink flowers.

'Meteor' ht: 45cm *18in* dist: 45m *18in.* Carmine-red flowers.

The fleshy stems, leaves and flowers of all *spectabile* cultivars dry to a beautiful russet-brown that makes it hard to despatch them to the compost heap, even when the new shoots are starting to grow in spring.

Sidalcea malvaeflora Nec./Pol. H.
Jun.–Aug., full sun, semi-shade.
If you like hollyhocks but find them too tall for your garden, or you cannot grow them because of rust, that debilitating disease of hollyhocks, then the closely related Sidalceas are an excellent substitute, with their satiny pink, salmon or red flowers and large central boss of stamens smothered in pollen. Like the hollyhock, there is space and food enough for two or three bees to each flower. The flowers open progressively from the bottom of the 30–45cm (12–18in) flower spikes to give an extended flowering period. The upper leaves are rather grass-like, with shallow lobes, the lower ones are broader with larger lobes, rather like a rounded

S. reevsiana 'Rubella'

Scabious leaf. Saxifrages can also be raised from seed, now available from several seed companies.

'Croftway Red' ht: 1m *3ft* dist: 45–60cm *18–24in.* The deepest red of all cultivars.

'Lovliness' ht: 75cm *2.5in* dist: 45cm *18in.* Shell-pink flowers. A beautiful cultivar.

'Rose Queen' ht: 1.25m *4ft* dist: 1m *3ft.* Clear rose-pink flowers.

'William Smith' ht: 1m *3ft* dist: 45–60cm *18–24in.* Salmon-pink flowers.

Skimmia Nec./Pol. Shr. ht: 90cm *3ft* dist: 60–90cm *2–3ft* Mar.–Apr., salt tol, semi-shade, shade.
All species and cultivars of this slow-growing, delightfully neat evergreen are excellent early spring sources of nectar. Only some, however, produce pollen, for the plants are usually of separate sexes. The quantities of pollen carried in the small four–five petalled male flowers, carried in terminal clusters, are truly prodigious and provide a rich feast for the bees. If weather conditions are suitable, the female plants compensate aesthetically for their lack of pollen by bearing clusters of large, bright-red, pea-sized berries, provided there is a male plant nearby. Odd berries may persist right through the winter, until the bushes come into flower again. The leaves are up to 10cm (4in) in length and emit a distinctive aroma when bruised, neither pleasant nor unpleasant. Unless otherwise stated, plant separate male and female plants if berries are required.

S. japonica A very variable species, probably due to the fact that it is often raised from seed. Can vary from 1–1.5m (3–5ft) in height.

'Foremanii' A very free-flowering form with large clusters of fruits.

'Fragrans' Like 'Rubella' this is an excellent pollinator and more free-flowering than any other species or cultivar, with the most wonderful fragrance imaginable from its greenish-white flowers.

'Rubella' The large clusters of bright-red flower buds are carried right through the late autumn and winter and, unlike fruits, they are not taken by the birds. Providing pollen, nectar and winter colour, this must be one of the very best all-round garden and bee plants, and it will serve as a good pollinator for 'Foremanii'.

S. reevsiana syn. *fortunei* acid. There is no need for a pollinator for this slightly tender species. The fruits are a matt crimson-red, and are very persistent.

Solidago (Golden Rod) Nec./Pol. H.

Aug.–Sep., full sun.

These tough, easily grown plants have plume-like inflorescences made up of small yellow flowers, held well above the leaves. These original types are not often seen in gardens now, since there are many newer, more compact and floriferous cultivars available, but they have naturalised themselves quite happily on waste ground and by the side of railway tracks, where they are eagerly sought out by honey bees.

The bulk of the species are from North America, where they are regarded as important bee plants, but Solidago *virgaurea* is widely distributed in Britain and Europe. It is of particular use to the bees since it has a very long flowering season – June to September – but has little merit as a garden plant. The leaves of all species are rather narrow, almost lance-shaped.

'Cloth of Gold' ht: 45cm *18in* dist: 30cm *1ft*. Deep-yellow flowers.

'Golden Shower' ht: 75cm *2.5ft* dist: 60cm *2ft*. The deep-yellow flower plumes of this cultivar are more arching and informal than many others.

'Golden Thumb' ht: 30m *12in* dist: 23m *9in*. The leaves of this robust little plant take on some of the deep yellow flower colouration.

Sorbus Nec./Pol. T.
May–Jun., salt tol., full sun.

A decorative genus of trees and shrubs with so many attributes that every garden should have one, and since there are species that grow to no more than 45cm (18in) high there can be no excuse! They are all absolutely hardy, growing in the most exposed sites, and many are salt-spray resistant. The leaves are toothed and may be simple in shape, as in the *aria* (whitebeam) group, or much divided, rather like the dog rose, in the *aucuparia* (rowan or mountain ash) types. In many species and cultivars the autumn leaf colour can be quite breathtaking, with yellows, reds, coppers and combinations of all three colours on the same plant. Add to this the brilliant clusters of red, red-purple, white, pink, or yellow berries and you have a warming sight for the coldest of autumn days. The masses of flat-headed clusters of small white flowers are not unattractive and are worked with some enthusiasm (especially the whitebeam) by honey bees.

For some unknown reason the birds (which can strip a tree in the space of two or three hours) seem to prefer red and orange berries to yellow or white, and it is not uncommon to see white-berried species, such as *hupehensis* untouched in late January – an added bonus.

S. aria (Whitebeam) ht: 12m *40ft*. A beautifully proportioned tree with oval leaves up to 11.5cm (4.5in) long, the upper surfaces grey at first, turning green as they mature, intensely grey-white beneath. Good russet-gold autumn colour, and deep crimson berries. Rather too large for the average sized garden. The cultivar 'Lutescens' is more widely grown and has the upper leaf surfaces covered in dense creamy white hairs, turning grey in autumn.

AUCUPARIA TYPES (Dog Rose Leaves)

'Beissneri' ht: 9m *30ft*. An erect cultivar with beautiful, shiny copper-russet bark, which literally glows in even the weakest winter sunshine. The leaves are deeply toothed, almost 'ferny' and pale green, especially when young, the leaf stalks and stems of young shoots are a dull red. You may have difficulty in finding this cultivar in the average garden centre, but it is well worth seeking out.

'Fastigiata' ht: 4.5m *15ft*. An erect slow-growing tree with a compact growth habit and large bright-red fruits.

'Xanthocarpa' syn. 'Fructuluteo' ht: 9m *30ft* A cultivar with amber-yellow fruits.

S. cashmeriana ht: 4.5m *15ft*. The white flowers, flushed with pink, of this small graceful tree or large shrub are worked with great enthusiasm by bees. The elegant leaves have seventeen–nineteen strongly serrated leaflets and colour well in autumn. The glistening white drooping fruits are almost 1.3cm (0.5in) in diameter and hang on until well after the leaves have fallen.

S. hupehensis ht: 6m *20ft*. This species has white berries with a pink tinge. The branches are a distinct purplish-brown, the leaves have a bluish-green cast with good red autumn colouration.

'Joseph Rock' An outstanding cultivar with creamy-yellow fruits, but it is so susceptible to fireblight that it is probably not worth the risk of trying it in southern Britain or Europe, where the disease has reached epidemic proportions due to the milder climate.

S. reducta ht: 45cm *18in*. A dwarf suckering shrub, ideal for the rock or peat garden. The petioles are red and the leaflets shiny, turning reddish-purple to bronze in autumn. The small fruits are white flushed with pink.

S. sargentiana ht: 9m *30ft*. A superb species with leaves up to 30cm (1ft) in length, and large sticky buds, rather like those of the horse-chestnut, but bright red in colour. The scarlet autumn leaf colour is outstanding. The fruits are small but the clusters can be up to 15cm (6in) across.

S. vilmorinii ht: 3.5m *12ft*. An elegant, wide-spreading small tree or shrub. The dark-green fern-like leaflets, which number up to thirty-one, turn a reddish-purple in autumn. The loose clusters of berries are dark red at first, turning to pink and then white with a pink flush.

Stachys (Woundwort) Nec./Pol.
Full sun.
A handsome and distinctive genus of plants, of which there are several species native to Britain and Europe. Two of these, *S. sylvatica* (Wood Woundwort) and *S. germanica* (Downy Woundwort) are worth growing in their own right.

The upright square-stemmed flower spikes that are so typical of Labiatae bear whorls of distinctly two-lipped flowers. The narrow flower tubes rarely exceed 6mm (0.25in) and thus allow easy bee access. All species thrive on poor dry soils.

S. byzantina syn. *lanata* (Lambs' Ears) H. ht: 23cm *9in* Jul.–Sep. One of the best and most easily grown of all ground-cover plants. The narrowly elliptic leaves generally persist through the winter and are covered on both surfaces with perhaps the most dense woolly hair of any plant. They are irresistible to the touch and feel softer than down. The pale-lavender flowers that peep through the woolly calyces look absolutely right. No wonder Gertrude Jekyll used this marvellous plant so freely.
   The cultivar 'Silver Carpet', which looks very similar, rarely flowers, so if you are uncertain of the identity of a plant, check for flower spikes in August before purchasing.

S. grandiflora syn. *Betonica macrantha* (Betony) H. ht: 45cm *18in* May–Jun. A distinctly different plant to *byzantina*, with no hair present on leaves or stems. The leaves are up to 7.5cm (3in) long, ovate with nicely scalloped edges, and also deeply veined. Flowers purple. The cultivar 'Rosea' has pink flowers.

Stranvaesia Nec./Pol. Shr.
Jun.–Jul., full sun, semi-shade.
A handsome vigorous evergreen, rather similar to the Cotoneasters and, like them, very susceptible to fireblight. The leaves are lance-like and leathery, up to 12.5cm (5in) long. The leaf stalks and new buds area very attractive burgundy-red, particularly during the winter months, and as the leaves are quite close together this is a very distinctive feature. Some of the leaves also take on a red colouration, particularly during cold weather, and this adds to the winter display.
   The creamy-white flowers are carried profusely in loose clusters on short side shoots and are followed by crimson fruits fully 9mm (0.33in) across, which hang late in to the winter since birds do not seem to favour them as food. The flowers are extremely attractive to all bees and will be covered in bumble- and honey bees collecting both nectar and pollen.

S. davidiana

S. davidiana ht: 4.5m *15ft* dist: 2.5–3m *8–10ft*. The flowers are white but have red anthers. You may see *salicifolia* offered in garden centres, and there is little difference between this and *davidiana*, both producing some very stiffly erect branches.

S. undulata ht: 2.5m *8ft* dist: 2–2.5m *6–8ft*. Rather more spreading in habit, often growing wider than it does high. The leaves are usually wavy at the margins.

Symphoricarpos (Snowberry) Nec./Pol. Shr.
Full sun, shade.
This is a 'grow anywhere' shrub with a most invasive suckering habit. Left unchecked a single plant will in about ten years cover 45m (50 yards) or so of ground. However, if it is kept under control twice a year, by removing suckers and spreading branches, it is a most rewarding shrub. The rounded leaves are carried on slender twiggy shoots that are so much characteristic of this genus, mid-green above, pale beneath.

S. albus (Snowberry) ht: 2m *6ft* dist: 2–2.5m *6–8ft*. A North American plant that has naturalised itself happily more or less throughout Europe in hedgerows and waste places, and you must be vigilant if you do not want it to take over.

S. x chenaultii 'Hancock' ht: 1m *3ft* dist: 1.25m *4ft*. The absolute maze of prostrate stems that this hybrid builds up never ceases to amaze me, with a capacity to smother out any weed seeds that are unlucky enough to find themselves beneath its branches. The berries are purple to white. The other hybrids and cultivars tend not to produce suckers, so are less invasive.

S. x doorenbosii 'Magic Berry' ht: 1m *3ft* dist: 1.25m *4ft*. Rose-pink berries very freely produced.

'Mother of Pearl' ht: 1m *3ft* dist: 1.25m *4ft*. Pink berries.

'White Hedge' ht: 1.25m *4ft* dist: 1.25–1.5m *4–5ft*. White berries carried freely.

Syringa (Lilac) Nec./Pol. Shr.
Full sun, semi-shade.
The glorious fragrance of the dense flower clusters of lilac in the May garden is unmistakable. In many, but not all species the tubes of the four-petalled flowers are too long for the honey bee to gain access to the nectar. But, being narrow, nectar 'flooding' can quickly take place in sunny weather, thus allowing partial access at least. The flowers of many of the cultivars grown are double and must constitute the ultimate frustration for bees: nectar out of reach and no pollen!

Choose only those forms with single flowers and short tubes, if you want the best of both worlds. Also, consider carefully if you are prepared to make room for what are mostly quite large plants with relatively short flowering periods, with little else to offer, the leaves producing little in the way of summer attraction or autumn colour.

Flowering at the same time as many Rhododendrons, and with a similar colour range, lilacs should be grown in their stead if the soil is alkaline, for they will thrive as very few other plants can at a high pH. To ensure a good display in successive years, cut off the old flower spikes as soon as they fade.

S. microphylla 'Superba' ht: 2m *6ft* dist: 1.25m *4ft* Apr.–May and Aug. With its small oval leaves and slender branches this is not at all a typical lilac. The rosy-lilac flower clusters are relatively small and erect, and with its longer-than-average flowering season and neat habit this is an excellent bee and garden plant.

S. velutina syn. *palabiniana* ht: 1.25m *4ft* dist: 1.25m *4ft* May–Jun. The velvety dark-green leaves of this dwarf species are quite distinct, and beautifully complement the pale lavender-pink flowers.

S. x prestoniae ht: 3.5m *12ft* dist: 3.5m *12ft* May–Jun. The individual flowers of this vigorous hybrid are small but are carried in their thousands. There is a range of cultivars available, all of which have predominantly darkish-pink to burgundy-red flowers. A magnificent plant if you have the space, the purple buds providing their own display during May, before the flowers open.

S. vulgaris ht: 3m *10ft* dist: 2.5m *8ft* May–Jun. This is the familiar common lilac, parent of so many of the garden cultivars and hybrids. Those listed all have single flowers.

'Marachel Foch' Bright carmine-rose flowers.

'Maud Notcutt' Very large white flowers.

'Primrose' Yellow flowers.

'Souvenir de Louis Spaeth' Deep wine-red flowers.

Thymus (Thyme) Nec. Shr.
Dry, full sun.
A wonderful genus of dwarf erect or carpeting herbs or shrubs, with strongly aromatic foliage and pink or mauve flowers. The prostrate types are ideal for 'gaps' in paved areas or rock-garden paths, where they yield up their spicy aroma with each step taken. They are also ideal 'cascade' plants for walls and rocks. They will need to be taken in hand when grown in company with other alpines, for they are invasive and will surround and swamp any of their weaker companions.

The individual flowers are tiny, less than 6mm (0.25in), and distinctly two-lipped, the upper notched, the lower divided into three. The flowers open progressively from the base of the rounded heads or spikes. In just one such 8mm (0.33in) head, I have counted thirty-eight individual flowers, and on the species in question, *T. leucotrichus*, the flower heads are so close that there are no leaves in sight at all. There must, therefore, be around 50,000 flowers during the season for my bees, in just one square foot of plant!

The Thymes are certainly excellent bee plants and are widely distributed in the wild, especially in the southern parts of Europe where considerable crops of Thyme honey are taken – some, such as Mount Hymettus honey, being world famous. The three species commonly found wild in Britain are also happiest in the south, since they all really prefer dryish conditions. Many of the excellent golden and silver foliage types do not flower freely enough to warrant mention here.

T. serpyllum syn. *praecox arcticus* ht: 7.5m *3in*. This species includes most of the more commonly grown Thymes.

'Albus' dist: 1–1.25m *33–4ft* Jun.–Aug. Deep-green foliage with white flowers. Rampant.

Thymus 'Doone Valley' Thyme

'Coccineus Major' dist: 60cm *2ft* Jun.–Aug. Dark foliage and crimson flowers.

'Doone Valley' dist: 23cm *9in* Jul.–Oct.
A beautiful cultivar with dark-green leaves irregularly splotched with gold. The pale lavender flower heads are its crowning glory, and there can be no finer colour combination of leaves and flowers in the whole plant kingdom.

'Pink Chintz' dist: 60cm *2ft* Jun.–Aug. Salmon-pink flowers.

T. languinosus ht: 10cm *4in* dist: 1m *3ft* Jun.–Aug. Grey-green leaves with long hairs, particularly at the edges. Vigorous.

T. leucotrichus ht: 23cm *9in* dist: 30cm *1ft* May–Aug. Dark grey-green leaves and pink flowers in profusion, before any other species is even showing bud colour.

T. necifferi ht: 7.5cm *3in* dist: 45cm *18in* Jun.–Aug. Narrow grey hairy leaves and pink flowers carried on long trailing shoots. Quite different from the other species.

Tilia (Lime or Linden) Nec./Pol. T.
Full sun, semi-dry.
With the demise of the elm in western Europe the lime is once more in the ascendant as an avenue, hedge and general park and estate tree. This is good news for bees, for the lime is a most important source of nectar in some areas of Britain,

for example around Birmingham and London, but in most other areas of Britain little nectar is obtained from these trees. The sweetly fragrant flowers are in pendant clusters, and the flower stalks are attached to the 5–7.5cm (2–3in) pale-green bracts which are such a distinctive feature of all limes. Lime honey has a very pleasant slightly minty flavour and a greenish tinge to its colour. A small quantity of pollen is obtained, but bees seem to have trouble in collecting it.

Like some other trees, limes carry a host of aphids during the summer, and these secrete quantities of sticky honeydew over the leaves. This is used as food by the aptly named sooty mould, which can often be seen covering the leaves with black smudges in late summer. Honeydew is also collected by the honey bee, yielding a honey which can vary from golden to almost black in colour, with a rich flavour particularly reminiscent of dried figs in the darker samples. Some honeydew honeys are much prized, the best known being Black Forest Pine honey, which is produced from the exudation of the pine aphids.

The nectar of some lime species, particularly *petiolaris*, *x euchlora*, *tomentosa* and *orbicularis*, can at times stupefy and even kill bees, and it has been suggested by those who have access to large collections of different species of lime that to a certain extent all have some degree of toxicity. The toxicity seems to vary from year to year, and to affect bumble-bees with greater severity than honey bees.

If you have a large garden and the patience to wait twelve–fifteen years for the first flowers, then you might like to try one of the less vigorous species listed.

T. miqueliana ht: 6–9m *20–30ft* Aug. A slow-growing, late-flowering species. The broad and slightly lobed leaves are carried well into the autumn.

T. platyphyllos 'Laciniata' ht: 4.5–6m *15–20ft* Jul. Leaves deeply serrated.

Tradescantia (Spiderworts) Nec./Pol. H.
ht: 60cm *2ft* dist: 45cm *18in* Jun.–Oct., full sun, semi-shade.
Erect herbaceous plants with many long, narrow leaves sticking out in all directions, often almost at right angles to the stem. The rather flat three-petalled flowers are carried in terminal clusters and may be up to 5cm (2in) across, in a wide range of colours. The stamens are attractively bearded and the six anthers are a quite bright yellow. The flowering period is long in any reasonable soil. All the following are cultivars of *x andersonii* (previously *virginiana*).

'Isis' Oxford-blue flowers.

'Osprey' The flowers are pure white with a pale-lavender 'beard'.

'Purewell Giant' Bright-carmine flowers.

'Purple Dome' Deep violet-blue flowers.

Tricyrtis Nec. H.
Sep.–Oct., full sun, semi-shade.
Toad Lily is not the most alluring name for a plant with such pretty flowers. The plant takes this name from the three swollen nectaries at the base of the flowers, which are carried singly or in groups, and are variously and distinctly spotted according to species. The six pointed tepals are fused at the base, but then flare out so that each can be seen quite separately. For the rest, the flowers are similar to those of the lilies. The root system is rhizomatous and does not always survive cold winters; some dry peat or leaves spread over the plants in November will afford a degree of protection.

Good drainage, coupled with a soil sufficiently high in organic matter to retain moisture, is essential for success.

T. formosana ht: 60cm *2ft* dist: 45cm *18in.* The erect flowers are pale purple with darker spots and a yellow throat. Leaves up to 12.5cm (5in) long.

T. hirta ht: 60cm *2ft* dist: 75cm *2.5ft.* Flowers erect, held close to the stem either solitary or in groups, white with purple spot. The white form 'Alba' is usually more dwarf.

Tulipa (Tulips) Pol. B./C.
Full sun.
The tulips are so well known as to require very little in the way of a detailed description. They range from the garish doubles and parrots, through the elegant, lily-flowered, to the dwarfer, more interesting and generally less vulgar species and their cultivars. These latter seem to be growing in popularity – an interesting backlash to the excesses of the plant breeders, and long may it continue.

The English national collection of tulip species is held at the University Botanic Garden, Cambridge, and is well worth a visit in spring. Unlike the more 'fancy' cultivars, the species and their cultivars could well do with a popularity boost. All look best when closely planted in groups, although they may be used in conjunction with dwarf spring bedding plants such as Arabis, Bellis or pansy.

Although tulips produce a mass of pollen, mostly yellow, they are not front-rank bee plants since they are not sought out when other more palatable sources are available. They do not, however, take up much space and may be a welcome change from the more normal yellow and blue spring bulb colours.

Plant the bulbs 10–15cm (4–6in) deep in rock gardens or at the edge of shrub or herbaceous borders, where they will be able to dry out thoroughly during the summer. This 'baking' always seems to result in a better display of flowers the following spring.

T. clusiana (Lady Tulip) ht: 20cm *8in* dist: 10–15cm *4–6in* Apr. The outside of the petals is rose-red, the interior creamy-white, with a purple base. The leaves may be red-edged.

T. eichleri ht: 25cm *10in* dist: 10–15cm *4–6in* Apr. Scarlet petals with a shiny black base, margined with yellow.

T. fosteriana ht: 30cm *12in* dist: 10–15cm *4–6in* Apr. Large scarlet flowers with a black basal blotch, margined with yellow within. Several cultivars are available.

T. greigii ht: 20cm *8in* dist: 10–15cm *4–6in* May. There is a very wide range of these slightly later-flowering striped and marble-leaved cultivars. Some, such as 'Cape Cod' can be 45cm (18in) or so in height, but most of them average 20–25cm (8–10in).

T. kaufmanniana (Water-Lily Tulips) ht: 12.5–23cm *5–9in* dist: 10–15cm *4–6in* Mar. In common with other species, the bulbs of *kaufmanniana* do not need to be lifted annually, but unlike many of these other species, which tend to weaken in time, *kaufmanniana* proliferates and gets stronger each year. The number of cultivars is legion and most of them have their large leaves attractively splotched and marbled with dull purple.

T. praestans 'Fusilier' ht: 25cm *10in* dist: 10–15cm *4–6in* Apr. One to six orange-scarlet flowers are produced on each stem of this very showy cultivar. Grow it in a sunny border with pink Helianthemums, the first flowers of which start to appear in late April, just as those of the tulip have passed their best.

T. humilis syn. *pulchella* ht: 10cm *4in* dist: 10cm *4in* Mar. A red dwarf with flowers which may vary in colour from very pale pink to crimson and even dull red-purple. The blotch at the base of the petals may be yellow or black.

T. tarda ht: 12.5cm *5in* dist: 10cm *4in* Apr. There are three–six white star-shaped flowers with a broad variable green stripe, edged with yellow, on the exterior. The whole of the centre of the flower is yellow, producing rather a 'fried egg' effect. A very pretty flower indeed.

Ulex (Gorse, Furze or Whin) Nec./Pol. Shr.
Dry, salt tol., full sun.
Rather than dismiss this somewhat antisocial plant that grows wild anyway, pause – for there is a dwarf form, and the gorse has many attributes, one of which (its ability to produce some flowers every day of the year) is very rare. The musky flower scent is also quite addictive, particularly when the bushes are in full flower,

covered with showers of the chrome-yellow pea-like flowers. Gorse thrives on the very poorest of soils (as evidenced by its frequent presence on heathland areas), and needs no pruning, fertilisers or fuss. It is quite a popular bee plant and does produce enormous amounts of pollen. In common with most other legumes gorse does not like root disturbance, so buy a pot-grown plant or collect some of the black-brown pods and sow their seeds in situ; they are easily raised from seed.

U. europaeus ht: 2m *6ft* dist: 1.25–2m *4–6ft* Mar–May. The common gorse of British heathlands.

U. minor ht: 60cm *2ft* dist: 60cm *2ft* Jul.–Oct. Autumn flowering, with paler yellow small flowers.

Verbascum (Mullein) Nec./Pol. H.
Jun.–Aug., full sun.

From a basal rosette of ovate to lance-shaped leaves, which in many species are covered with soft hairs, the mulleins produce their stiffly erect single or branched flower spikes. These will persist for years if not cut down after flowering, particularly in a hot dry climate, where they are often a distinctive feature of the landscape. A second flush of slower spikes – somewhat shorter – will often be produced in September, October or even November if the old spikes are cut back as soon as they finish flowering. The flower spikes are packed with the shallowly cupped flowers (similar to Potentilla) about 3.5cm (1.5in) in diameter, each with five lobes; the 'bottom' lobe is central and is larger than the other four. The five stamens are densely covered with soft white hairs, giving the flower centre a very woolly appearance, and from their 'wool' the bright-orange anthers peep. The single stigma seems to push through at any angle where there is a gap in the hairs. The bases of the petals are also hairy.

Few of the Verbascums are long-lived, and replacement within two years may prove necessary. They do tend to seed themselves reasonably freely, so these seedlings could act as the replacements, but some variation in shape, size and colour should be expected. Taking cuttings of basal shoots that have not flowered is another alternative and the new plants will be exactly the same as the parents.

Good drainage is essential, and it does not really seem to matter how dry the soil becomes. Several species are found growing in the wild in Britain, particularly in the south and southeast on calcareous soils. There are even more species in southern Europe, particularly the Mediterranean regions.

V. bombyciferum ht: 1.5m *5ft* dist: 60–90cm *2–3ft*. A handsome plant, covered with a dense felt of silver hair, and with leaves over 30cm (1ft) long. The flowers are bright yellow. 'Silver Spire', is paler than the type and available from some seedsmen, and is not a difficult plant to raise.

V. chaixii syn. *vernale* ht: 1m *3ft* dist: 45cm *18in*. Yellow flowers with purple stamens.

V. dumulosum ht: 30cm *12in* dist: 30cm *12in*. White-felted leaves, and yellow flowers with purple stamens. Needs a sheltered spot or some other form of winter protection.

V. x 'Letitia' ht: 23cm *9in* dist: 23cm *9in*. Masses of bright-yellow flowers, leaves covered with silvery hairs.

V. phoenicum ht: 1.25m *4ft* dist: 60cm *2ft*. Many of the cultivars and hybrids in cultivation are derived from this species.

'Bridal Bouquet' White flowers blushed with pink.

'Cotswold Queen' Buff flowers.

'Gainsborough' Flowers a bright canary yellow.

'Hartley' Multi-coloured flowers of buff and plum-purple.

'Pink Domino' Darker leaved and slightly shorter than the cultivars listed above, with rose-pink flowers.

Veronica (Speedwell) Nec./Pol. H.
Full sun, semi-shade.
All the speedwells have short or long flower spikes and a very long flowering season, making them both elegant and desirable as garden plants, eagerly sought out by honey bees whenever and wherever they are in flower. The individual flowers have four or five widely spreading lobes, each conspicuously veined in a darker shade of the ground colour. The flower tube is short and a ring of hairs in the pale eye protects the nectar at the base of the ovary. The two stamens stick out from the petticoat – like flowers with two legs, with the anthers as feet.

Tall and dwarf species have been separated on the opposite page.

✓ **Viburnum** Nec./Pol. Shr.
Full sun.
A very hardy and easily grown genus of plants containing a large number of species and cultivars, amongst which are some of the best of all garden shrubs. The small, five-petalled tubular flowers, which make up the often flat or rounded flower heads, are in many cases deliciously fragrant and may be followed by showy fruits.

TALL SPECIES

With their long elegant flower spikes these all contrast well with plants of rounded form.

V. gentianoides ht: 60cm *2ft* dist: 45cm *18in* May–Jun. This has spikes of pale-blue flowers, 25cm (10in) long, 1.3cm (0.5in) or so across, and broadly oblong leaves. The variegated form has an irregular white edging to the leaves, and is a first-class plant, slightly less vigorous than the type.

V. longifolia 'Foersters Blue' ht: 50cm *2ft* dist: 45cm *18in* Jul.–Sep. Deep-blue flowers.

V. spicata ht: 45cm *18in* dist: 30cm *1ft* Jun.–Jul. Spikey blue flowers.

'Blue Fox' Deep-blue flowers.

'Red Fox' Crimson flowers.

V. spicata incana Silvery foliage with deep-blue flowers, variable when raised from seed.

V. teucrium 'Crater Lake Blue' ht: 30cm *1ft* dist: 23cm *9in* Jul.–Sep. A superb plant with dense spikes of deep-blue flowers.

V. virginica ht: 1.25m *4ft* dist: 1m *3ft* Aug.–Oct. Long, elegant flower spikes of very pale blue. The form 'Alba' has white flowers.

DWARF SPECIES

Very easily grown plants, ideal for the rock garden, scree or border, spreading quickly to give excellent ground cover.

V. prostrata 'Blue Sheen' ht: 23cm *9in* dist: 30cm *1ft* May–Jun. Powder-blue flowers.

'Trehane' Golden leaves and deep-blue flowers.

V. spicata incana 'Nana' ht: 23cm *9in* dist: 30cm *1ft* Jul.–Sep. A dwarf version of *spicata incana* (see above).

The almost irresistible germander speedwell *(V. chamaedrys)* should be admired in the wild, for it is virtually impossible to get rid of once it has established itself in a lawn or border. It is certainly a lovely sight, with its deep-blue flowers in early March.

Viburnum *tinus*

The evergreen Viburnums generally have large heavily veined leaves, the deciduous species in many cases give good autumn colour effects. Nectar production can be very variable, especially on the winter-flowering species.

V. x bodnantense 'Dawn' ht: 3m *10ft* dist: 2.5–3m *8–10ft* Nov.–Mar. Clusters of fragrant deep-pink flower buds, opening to paler pink before any leaves appear, make this one of the best winter-flowering shrubs.

V. carlesii ht: 1.25m *4ft* dist: 1.25m *4ft* Apr.–May. A deservedly popular shrub with pale green leaves that colour well in autumn, and clusters of pink sweetly fragrant flowers. These open to white, and are followed by small black fruits. The cultivar 'Aurora' is redder in bud and opens to pink, with the same delicious fragrance.

V. davidii ht: 1m *3ft* dist: 1.25m *4ft* May–Jun., salt tol. A marvellous ground-cover plant with deep-green, heavily veined elliptical leaves which may be up to 15cm (6in) in length. The leaf stalks (particularly in winter) turn dull burgundy red, as do the flower buds that sit waiting all winter long for warm early summer weather before they open. The flowers are white and dainty.

The female plants, which you will not particularly want, occasionally bear small turquoise fruits which contrast beautifully with the dark-green foliage. Few garden centres label their plants male and female, so you will either have to take pot luck or inspect the plants in flower.

V. farreri syn. *fragrans* ht: 2.5m *8ft* dist: 2–2.5m *6–8ft* Nov.–Mar. Similar erect habit to *x bodnantense*, but the very fragrant flowers are much paler in colour and the spring 'flushes' are accompanied by the pale coppery-green embryo leaves, which give it an added attraction. It looks particularly good when planted against a dark background such as a conifer.

V. opulus 'Compactum' ht: 1.25m *4ft* dist: 1m *3ft* May–Jun. A nice dwarf form of the rather larger guelder rose with sharply toothed maple-like leaves. The white flower heads are composed of showy ray florets which surround the inner fertile flowers. Large bunches of glistening red fruits follow in autumn.

The cultivar 'Xanthocarpum' has golden translucent fruits, and the two cultivars planted together look very good when in fruit.

V. plicatum 'Mariesii ht: 2.25m *7ft* dist: 2.25–2.5m *7–8ft* May. Flat tiers of branches covered in snow-white flowers make this an outstanding garden plant, which even when not in flower remains of interest for the way it contrasts with other plant forms.

V. rhytidophyllum ht: 3.5m *12ft* dist: 3m *10ft* May–Jun. A fast-growing shrub with large dark-green, heavily veined leaves, white-felted beneath. These can look very sad and drooping in the winter, especially during prolonged cold periods, but they soon recover on warm sunny days. The felt-covered flower buds, after sitting still all winter, finally open in late spring to large 15cm (6in) dull-white flower heads. The fruits are small, red at first then black. A really bold plant for the larger garden.

V. tinus ht: 2.75m *9ft* dist: 2.25–2.5m *7–8ft* Nov.–May. The Laurustinus, as it is commonly known, is perhaps the most commonly planted of the Viburnums. Its dark evergreen leaves are one of its major attractions. For the bees, it is the round pink-budded flower heads which open to white from early winter to spring that make it a favourite. The small blue-black whortleberry-like clusters of fruits are most attractive and are often still present when the new flowers open. The cultivar 'Eve Price' is slightly less vigorous and has smaller leaves. In less exposed and severely cold districts the variegated form, 'Variegatum', is worth a try and is a genuinely showy plant with creamy yellow leaves.

Viola (Pansies and/or Violets) Nec.
The larger-flowered garden types are generally known as pansies, the smaller ones are often referred to as violets, but there are no hard and fast distinctions. All have rather flat, nodding or horizontal flowers, often fragrant, with velvet-textured conspicuously veined petals. The flowers, with their hairy throats and finger-like nectaries tucked away to the side and base of the stamens, make

honey bee access to nectar anything but easy, but they are worked by bees, especially those plants with short nectary spurs.

Most of the pansies have a small eye in a contrasting colour, and some are cultivated specifically for their face-like or fringe markings, in a variety of colours. The summer-flowering cultivars, although very showy, will not be first choice for the honey bee when there is a wide choice of other flowers, so they are not described here.

'Universal' Bien. ht: 23cm *9in* dist: 23cm *9in* Sep.–May, full sun, semi-shade. The 'Universal' range is quite outstanding and given a relatively mild winter will produce 7.5–10cm (3–4in) flowers continuously for twelve months. The colour range is good and there are separate white, apricots, blues (pale and dark), yellows, purples and reds. 'Apricot' is a particular favourite, with its rich deep colouration.

'Floral Dance' Bien. ht: 23cm *9in* dist: 23cm *9in* Sep.–May, full sun, semi-shade. Flowers somewhat smaller. Available in a wide range of colours, all with a largish irregular black eye.

Both the above cultivars should be sown outdoors or under glass in May/June, for planting out in their final locations in September/October. The violets are rather more subtle than the pansies, and conjure up pictures of deliciously fragrant Mothers' Day posies edged with primroses.

V. cornuta H. ht: 10cm *4in* dist: 23cm *9in* Apr.–Sep., semi-shade. Available in white, pale-blue and dark-purple forms, flowering from spring to late autumn.

V. cucullata 'Freckles' H. ht: 15cm *6in* dist: 23cm *9in* Apr.–May, semi-shade. Very pale blue ground colour, almost covered with small purple freckles. A really stunning colour combination. It is difficult to believe that each flower has not been painstakingly hand-painted.

V. odorata (Sweet Violet) H. ht: 10cm *4in* dist: 15cm *6in* Apr.–May, semi-shade. The fragrance and deep-violet colour of the flower are simply incomparable. Several named cultivars are available.

V. labradorica 'Purpurea' H. ht: 10cm *4in* dist: 23–30cm *9–12in* dry, semi-shade. Lilac-mauve flowers set against dark-purple leaves. Handsome, but can be invasive.

Weigela Nec. Shr.
Full sun, semi-shade.
One of the earliest of the summer-flowering shrubs to show its colour, which it does year after year without any fuss. Clusters of funnel-shaped flowers, each

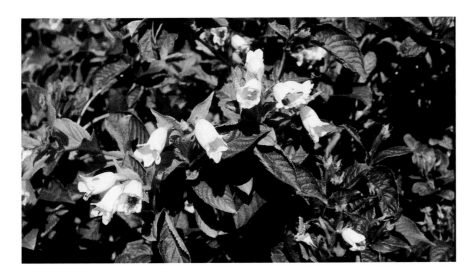

Weigela *middendorffiana*

with their Fuchsia-like pistil and great knob-like stigma. A smaller, second flush of flowers may be produced in the autumn. The flower tubes are wide enough for honey bee access, but they may gain entry from the side through holes made by bumble-bees. Flower size will deteriorate if the plants are left unpruned, thus making bee access more difficult, so thin out the old flowered shoots in February each year.

W. florida ht: 2m *6ft* dist: 2m *6ft* May–Jun. Flower buds rose-pink at first, paler within.

'Foliis Purpureis' ht: 1.25m *4ft* dist: 1.25m *4ft* May–Jun. Slower growing than the species, its attractive dark-purple foliage contrasts nicely with the deep-pink flowers. It looks particularly good when planted next to variegated shrubs. Plant this cultivar next to 'Variegata'.

'Variegata' ht: 1.25m *4ft* dist: 1.25m *4ft* May–Jun. This must be one of the very best variegated shrubs, with its wide creamy-yellow leaf variegation which in cold weather may partially turn a delicate pink. Flowers pale pink.

W. x 'Bristol Ruby' ht: 1.25m *4ft* dist: 1.25m *4ft* May–Jun. Brilliant ruby-red flowers. A superb plant, winner of the Royal Horticultural Society's ultimate accolades: Award of Merit and Award of Garden Merit.

W. middendorffiana ht: 1.25m *4ft* dist: 1.25m *4ft* Apr.–May. Yellow foxglove-like flowers, unusual in the genus, with dark orange markings on the lower lobes. Needs some shelter from wind and sun.

Above: Close-up of a small swarm
Far right: This garden contains many herbaceous plants to interest the bees from the two traditional skeps (labelled 'hives') at the top of the picture

A Beekeeper's Garden

If you enjoy seeing the bees in your garden, you may want to go a step further and keep bees. Colonies of honey bees can be kept successfully anywhere: beekeeping is practised from the centre of the largest cities to the depths of the countryside.

If you do keep honey bees the most important consideration must always be that the bees are not a nuisance to neighbours or the public passing by. There is no reason why they should be; honey bees do not interfere with anyone when they are away from the hive. They are defending the colony when they cause trouble, and conditions should be so arranged that their instinct to defend is not aroused. If a quiet strain of bee is correctly sited and looked after with care and consideration for neighbours as well as the welfare of the colonies, and the number of colonies installed kept at a reasonable level, then there is no reason why the neighbours should come into contact with the bees at all. Strains of honey bees can be obtained which are so quiet that they will not try to sting the beekeeper when the colony is being taken apart during manipulation. These strains have to be looked for, so seek advice from an experienced beekeeper in your area to find out where the local sources are. Let no one convince you that bad-tempered bees make most honey, it is quite untrue.

Of the many hundreds of strains of honey bees that I have worked with, the two finest, both for honey production and quality of colony, were so quiet that they did not sting unless trapped and squeezed, inside a sleeve for instance. Good-quality, hardworking and quiet strains of honey bees can be obtained, and are a pleasure to work with.

FIRST GET YOUR BEES

The new beekeeper can start up in one of three ways: by buying a colony of bees, or a nucleus of bees, or by obtaining a swarm of bees.

Start with a nucleus bought from a reputable beekeeper or equipment supplier. A full-sized colony is an awesome sight to a tyro, no matter how docile it is, and a swarm is usually of unknown origin and you do not know what you are taking home: their temper may leave a lot to be desired, and they could be diseased.

A nucleus is a complete little colony which will not overawe the beginner; buy from a reputable source to ensure the nucleus will be docile, easy to handle and

free of important diseases. As the nucleus grows larger and becomes a colony, so will your ability to handle bees and your understanding of bee behaviour, so that hiccoughs which might happen in the early days that can be rather off-putting will seem normal and not a worry.

WHERE TO PUT THE HIVES

When you bring a colony of honey bees into your garden you must first decide where to site them. If you are a new beekeeper there are a number of things about the behaviour of bees that are important to understand. The colony must be brought in from at least three miles away, otherwise your bees will fly over some of the landmarks they flew over from their previous site, and this will cause them to follow their old flight lines to their former home. Honey bees do not orient afresh each time they leave the hive, it is not necessary in natural conditions, where they will be in a hollow tree or a cavity in a cliff, which is certainly not going to move around. They learn the position of their colony during the first few days of their lives, and that is sufficient in natural conditions.

Bees belonging to a beekeeper may be subjected to having their colony moved around, sometimes over considerable distances, and have to reorient and learn a new set of flight lines each time they are moved. Many of the older bees may rush out of the hive without realising they are in a new place and be lost, unable to find their way to the new home. To mitigate this effect, lightly stuff the entrance of a newly moved hive with fresh green grass, which will emphasise to the bees that something is different. It will slow up exit from the hive until the grass has withered and the bees can clear it away.

Once honey bees have flown from a new position they will have learned their new flight lines and local landmarks, and will accurately return to the hive entrance. Should you then decide the hive would be better in a different position in the garden, and move it ten feet or more, the bees going out will not realise they have been moved and on the return journey will use the flight lines they have just learned, returning to the place where the hive entrance was before it was moved. Many will cluster on the ground at this spot, and die. The particular strain of bee affects how many will fail to find their hive which is close by, but in any case many will be lost and the colony will be considerably set back in development. The old beekeeping rule that 'Bees should be shifted under three feet or over three miles' is a good one to remember and follow.

So when you bring a nucleus or colony of honey bees into the garden, you must put it on its permanent site before the bees are allowed to fly. You cannot put them somewhere 'for the time being' while you make up your mind where they should be permanently placed. If you do, you will have the job of shifting them three feet a day until they are in the right place, or have to leave them where they are until winter when, after a week or two of very cold weather, when the bees have not flown, it is possible to shift them across the garden to their new site.

Do not keep the bees confined in their box or hive until you have made up your mind. Colonies should be shut in for a short a time as possible, or many bees, or the whole colony, will die. Nuclei can be kept shut in for longer periods, but during this time they need careful attention. They should be kept in the cool and in the dark if possible, and when they begin to buzz loudly a cup or two of water should be poured, through the top screen, over the bees. It is better to decide on their position before they arrive, put them in the right place straight away, and open the box to let them fly.

Swarms brought into the garden must also be hived on their permanent site right away. They learn their new position as soon as they fly from a hive they have accepted as suitable. If there is something they do not like about the hive, or, more likely, if they are small swarms (called casts or afterswarms) which have come out of a colony several days after the first swarm has left, and usually contain more than one unmated queen, they will leave the hive and hang up again as a swarm. The first swarm out of a colony each year, the prime swarm, usually has the old mated queen from the colony and will settle happily into any hive provided. The main difference with swarms is that they can be hived at a new position in their original apiary, and only a few of the older bees will return home to their old colony. The bees' behaviour patterns cause them to stay in a new position once they have swarmed (although in nature they will usually fly some way away from their old colony before setting up home in a new cavity).

A new beekeeper bringing bees into the garden, or an established beekeeper moving to a new home, must first decide where the bees are to be sited and should, if possible, prepare the apiary site before the bees arrive. It will be much more difficult to work around the hives when they are in position. Establishing the apiary requires two decisions: the position of the apiary in the garden, and the layout of the hives in the apiary.

The size of the garden and the closeness of neighbouring houses will affect where you site the hives. The apiary should be enclosed by a hedge, and should be sited as far from neighbours as possible. A very large plot in a rural setting will pose no problem. The bees can be sited away from the boundaries and in a position where they cannot overlook the garden from the entrance of the hives. This can be made certain by a low hedge of about about 1m (3–4ft) high, which will also act as wind shelter for the colonies.

In a small suburban, or urban, garden it is best to enclose the colonies, or the garden, in a hedge about 2m (6ft) tall, which pushes the flight lines of the bees up, above head height, before they leave the garden. This is necessary because bees do fly into obstacles, particularly ones that are not always there, and people may think they are being attacked when it is a quite accidental collision. In heavily built-up areas, once the bees are pushed up by a high fence they will be kept high by the houses, and only those actually working the flowers will descend into the gardens. In a rural setting bees will fly low to the ground when it is windy, and will even fly around under the lee of a hedge to go through gaps

BEEKEEPING TERMS

colony – a unit containing at least six, but usually ten or eleven, combs covered by adult bees, including a laying queen honey bee, and containing all stages of the young ages – that is, larvae and pupae.

nucleus – a small colony usually containing four combs covered with bees, a young laying queen and young of all stages (the collective name for the young is 'brood').

swarm – a collection of bees, about 10,000 in number, and a queen, which has left a colony and is on its way to set up a new home. It has no combs or brood. The swarm can be collected by a beekeeper and given or sold to the new beekeeper.

or gateways in considerable density. This behaviour should be thought about when siting, taking care that this does not happen where roads, footpaths or other rights of way exist. It may be possible to produce a new gap for them to fly through in a more convenient place.

Temporary fences can be of wattle or a small-meshed plastic, such as greenhouse shading. These materials last a few years, giving time for hedging plants to be planted and to become established, and are very efficient in pushing the bees up and providing a windbreak. A living hedge, however, is the most attractive and efficient way of fencing off the apiary because hedges provide better conditions for the colonies than walls, as these produce considerable wind turbulence close by. Wind coming through a hedge reduces the strength of the turbulence and pushes it some way back from the hedge. If colonies are placed 1–1.25m (3–4ft) from the hedge, and with the entrance pointing at the hedge, the bees will have calm air in which to slow down and enter the hive.

HOW MANY COLONIES?

The number of colonies which may be kept in an apiary will depend upon the type of area, and the density of human population surrounding it. Two is the minimum number of colonies which may conveniently be kept, one colony on its own is a liability because when things go wrong, and they surely will, you have no resource with which to repair it. Mistakes or natural problems can often be repaired with two colonies by taking from the unaffected hive. Two is also the maximum if you are setting up a new garden apiary in a built-up area. Let your neighbours know you are keeping bees.

If two works well for you and your neighbours, move to four or five colonies, but this is about the maximum to be kept in a built-up area for two reasons. Firstly, above this number the bees become more generally visible as they search around the hives in times of little forage, take cleansing flights in spring (leaving little yellow spots on washing), and later in the season large numbers of young bees fly around to gain orientation or indulge in play flights.

The second reason is that there may be far more beekeepers around in the immediate area than you would imagine, and too high a density of bees will reduce the possible crops of honey for everyone. There is only a finite amount of nectar available in an area, and the ideal stocking rate will be one that is just able to harvest this nectar and turn it into honey; too many bees will reduce the crop per colony and increase the cost of production, and too few bees will fail to collect some of the nectar and leave it to be consumed by the yeasts which live in the nectaries. There is no way of calculating the potential of an apiary – it can only be tested by practical experience. Remember it can vary from year to year and during different times of the same year.

In rural districts, on larger plots of land, more colonies can be kept, the number depending upon the proximity of neighbours and on the overstocking problem, which will be affected by the land use of the immediate neighbourhood. Most experienced beekeepers will agree that the maximum number in a permanent apiary in most areas of Britain should not be greater than about twelve to fifteen colonies; in some areas agricultural practices have so reduced the density of bee forage throughout the year that it does not provide subsistence for more.

The size of the apiary and the way the colonies are set out within it will depend upon the number of colonies involved and the amount of spare land available. Ideally, the two-colony apiary should have the colonies 2m (6ft) apart to give the beekeeper room to work and perform manipulations such as artificial swarming, and have them facing in opposite directions to minimise the drifting of young bees into the wrong colony. This would require an area of 4 x 2m (18 x 6ft) inside the hedges. This may not be available, but get as near the ideal as possible.

As the number of colonies on a site gets larger the problem of drifting becomes more severe. It occurs mainly when young bees are out on orientation flights and fail to return to the right hive. This causes colonies to become unbalanced, reducing the average crop from the apiary, and rapidly spreads disease from colony to colony. It is at its greatest when colonies are sited in a straight line, all facing the same direction, and at a minimum when the hives are placed in a circle, all facing a slightly different aspect. Siting twelve colonies in a circle would require an apiary of some 9.5 x 9.5m (31ft square), or if arranged in two smaller circles an area of 8.8 x 5.5m (29 x 18ft) would suffice. When placed in two or more clumps of hives bees will drift to places where the picture they see is repeated; this happens to returning foragers as well as young bees, and can be reduced by planting single small trees or shrubs in the apiary to act as landmarks.

In all cases the hives should be arranged so that when you are working on one, with the hive open, you are not standing in the flight line of a nearby hive, or trouble will ensue, not necessarily to yourself if the bees are docile, but it may initiate robbing between colonies, especially towards the end of the honey flows. Particularly in the case of a large apiary, there should be a good hard path between it and the place where the honey is to be extracted, so that a wheelbarrow, or better still a small two-wheeled truck, can be used at harvest time to convey the full boxes from place to place.

WHAT SORT OF HIVE?

My own choice of hive would be the Modified Commercial, but certainly a single-walled hive and not the old-fashioned WBC. Although the latter may be more decorative, it is more conspicuous, takes up more room, both when manipulating and for storage of parts not in use (all the extra pieces have to go somewhere), and is not as flexible in use, needing modification before some manipulation techniques can be used.

Place the hives on stands and, to avoid backache and for ease of manipulation,

TREES AND SHRUBS

Be sure to choose trees that will not become giants, for your own, your neighbours' and your bees' sakes; remember that there are few plants that thrive in the dense shade beneath such trees, and even fewer that your bees will bother visiting under such circumstances, even if they are in flower.

Do not be tempted to plant trees in groups of three or five; settle instead for single specimens, preferably of erect habit, of a size that is in scale with your garden and this will allow you to grow semi-shade-tolerant plants such as *Mahonia* and *Hypericum* right up to the tree bases. No attempt has been made in the plant lists to indicate spacings for trees for this reason.

The same principles of scale apply equally to shrubs. Although lovely, there can be few gardens that can find space for two *Magnolia x soulangeana*.

at such a height that you can stand at ease with your knuckles resting on the top of the brood chamber. This allows you to remove combs from the brood chamber for examination without bending, and is conducive to good handling, with little jarring or crushing of bees to annoy the colony. There are many varieties of stands, a good choice is one made of 5 x 5cm (2 x 2in) pegs driven about 30cm (12in) into the ground, with rails of the same material nailed on the top. Single stands should have rails about 50cm (20in) long, double stands 1.3m (4.33ft) long. Double stands are the more stable and the most useful in the long run, and need support only one colony. The height of the stands should be about 40cm (16in), but should be adjusted to suit your height.

In Europe many beekeepers keep their colonies in 'bee houses'. This has not been practised much in Britain, although it was more popular a century or so ago, but it has been suggested as a suitable method of beekeeping for urban and suburban conditions. The suggestion has merit for several reasons: colonies are well protected and inconspicuous, but, more important, they can be manipulated at almost any time and in any weather. This has considerable advantage in a town garden, where it is essential to prevent colonies swarming and possibly annoying neighbours. Manipulations can thus be done on time and are not at the mercy of the weather. A small shed of about 8 x 6ft (2.5 x 2m) would house 3-6 colonies, 3 on each long side, and the construction of the bee entrance. Using ordinary hives, I prefer this to the continental method of placing the hives against the wall, which makes it difficult to separate the boxes when working the colonies.

WATER

Honey bees require a lot of water throughout the year, except when a nectar flow is in progress, when they have a surplus that has to be evaporated off. They need the water to add to the stored honey so that they can eat it and, in very hot weather, to cool the brood in the hive. They prefer to take the water from places where it is in small quantity and can warm up, and seem to prefer dirty water to clean. They make themselves unpopular with the owners of garden ponds and swimming pools from which they collect water.

It is essential, particularly in a built-up area, to provide the bees with a water source, and to see that they use it. Probably the best is a drum of water with a tap, or a small hole, which can dribble onto a sloping board with a herringbone arrangement of slats to guide the water. Bees can be enticed to use it by filling the drum with a very weak sugar solution, but once they have found it plain water is sufficient. Encourage moss to grow on the board so it will be more efficient in holding the water. You could build your own garden pond and put plenty of plants in it so that the bees would have plenty of surfaces to stand on while drinking, and not far to swim should they fall in. Introduce the bees to your pond by putting a few saucers of weak syrup around its edge to attract them.

Bees and Beekeeping

The three types of honey bee in a colony: the male drone on the left, the queen in the centre and a worker on the right

Practical methods of beekeeping are covered in *Guide to Bees and Honey* (Ted Hooper, 1997), so this chapter only gives a brief resumé of the life of the honey bee, the events of the beekeeping year and the time the beekeeper needs to spend working the colonies.

THE HONEY BEE'S LIFE

The honey bee starts off as an egg laid in one of the cells of the honey comb. The eggs are laid by the queen, which has the ability to fertilise the eggs or not as she lays them. Unfertilised eggs develop into males, called drones, fertilised eggs produce females. There are two sorts of honey bee female: a fully sexually developed female, the queen, and a smaller female, the worker, which is incapable of mating although in special circumstances can lay a few eggs – which develop into males. The two sorts of female are termed castes.

The queen mates during the first three weeks of her life, and is incapable of doing so again. She is mother of all the individuals in the colony, and can lay eggs at a rate of 2,000 or more a day during peak periods of laying. The eggs hatch in three days to produce larvae, legless white grubs curled up in the bottom of the cells. The larvae are fed by the worker bees and grow rapidly until, at the end of eight to ten days, depending upon sex and caste, they are sealed in the cells by the workers with a domed wax capping. The larvae change into pupae and emerge as adults a few days later.

The normal honey bee colony comprises one queen, a large number of workers and, during summer, 500 or so drones. The population of workers varies with the time of year, from 5,000 to 10,000 in winter and 30,000 to 60,000 in mid-summer. This fluctuation of population is a major economic feature of the honey bee colony in the temperate areas of the world. The large summer population can work the flowers and store a large amount of honey surplus to their immediate requirements. This store can then be used by a much smaller population to provide it with food during the winter when no, or a very few, flowers are available.

The workers, as their name implies, do all the work of the colony, doing indoor jobs for about their first twenty days, and then becoming foragers working in the field for the rest of their lives – about another fifteen days. During this indoor period they produce beeswax and use it to construct the comb; they feed the brood, eating pollen to produce a sort of 'bee milk'. Workers take the nectar from incoming foragers, and convert it into honey by evaporating off most of the water and converting complex sugars to more simple ones. By this contact with the foragers they are themselves stimulated to begin foraging on the same plants, going out with complete details of the forage, position and distance from the hive, and the taste, smell and sugar concentration of the nectar. Few bees look for flowers, most are directed by the 'bee dance' to a specific crop.

Foragers fly out to collect four substances. The first, nectar, is processed into honey, and both these substances are composed mainly of sugar and water, and provide the energy which the bee needs for its daily life. Some sugar is converted by glands into beeswax, and much is converted by muscles into heat to keep the colony warm. A smaller number of foragers collect the second substance, pollen, the main food of the bee, providing its proteins, vitamins and mineral requirements. A variable number of bees collect water with which to dilute the honey and to cool the hive, and some collect a substance from plant buds called propolis, or bee glue, which is used to varnish over the inside of the hive, stop up any holes and glue down anything movable. Workers will mount guard and defend the colony whenever this is necessary, but only when it is necessary. During quiet times there is little evidence of watchfulness.

At normal times the bees are inhibited from producing new queens by a glandular substance, termed 'queen substance', produced by the reigning queen. As the queen gets older her production of queen substance reduces, or as the colony grows in population the amount of substance is insufficient to keep the workers inhibited and they produce new queens, not in the normal hexagonal cells but in specially constructed, hanging, acorn-shaped queen cells. When this happens the colony can accept a new queen, the old one dying or being killed, or more frequently they split up and produce one or more new colonies. This is swarming. It is the only way a colony can reproduce and become two or more colonies. The old queen, being capable only of laying eggs but in no way being able to look after them, has to leave, accompanied by a good number of workers to set up a new colony in a new home. The normal procedure is for a swarm to come out of the hive and hang up near by for a time, while some workers fly off to find a suitable place to set up the new nest. Having found a new home the swarm flies off to it and becomes a new colony.

At the end of the season, when flowers become very scarce, the queen stops laying and the colony settles down to endure the winter. Towards the end of winter the queen starts laying once more, and when eventually spring flowers appear the colony beings to expand once again.

THE BEEKEEPER'S YEAR

The art of beekeeping is to work with the honey bee and use its inherent patterns of behaviour to persuade it along the lines you wish it to take. Persuasion rather than compulsion is the rule; it is difficult, and painful, to try to make a bee do anything it doesn't want to do.

The beekeeping year starts in September when the colonies are got ready for winter, aged queens are replaced and it is assured that the colonies have sufficient stores to last them through the winter: those that are short are topped up with sugar syrup. Having prepared them correctly for winter the colonies can be left untouched until the following spring. Except in special circumstances the hives will not be opened again until the weather has warmed up and temperatures have reached $50°F$ ($10°C$) once more. On a nice spring day the beekeeper will wear the protective veil, light the smoker and open the colonies to see how the bees are progressing. At this time of year the main job is to discover any problems the colonies may have, and to get rid of the cause and to build them up to optimum condition. As colonies expand, boxes of comb are added to the hive for the bees to spread into.

Once colonies are built up to full size they are then liable to swarm unless steps are taken to prevent this happening. Preparations within the colony for swarming can occur any time from the first week of April to the end of July, and the event itself will depend upon the timing of the local flowers and the constancy of their succession.

Methods of swarm prevention and control can be carefully studied in any good beekeeping textbook and should be used. It is essential for good relations with neighbours, and for the productivity of your colonies, that colonies are prevented from swarming, particularly in urban or suburban situations.

After the swarming period the colonies are given additional shallow supers to accommodate the honey, if there is a nectar flow on, until the flows peter out and no surplus is being stored. The supers of honey are cleared of bees and taken away for the honey to be extracted from the comb and put into containers for storage.

The colonies must be prepared for winter once more. On average, beekeepers check their colonies once every seven to ten days during the active season, whichever is most convenient, and this means that they see them opened about twelve to fourteen times in a year. A competent beekeeper should need more or less ten minutes to manipulate a colony, while two working together should need only three minutes. This is the minimum time needed. You may take longer while you are learning, or because you are interested in looking at things in the colony which are not really of practical importance in producing more honey. One thing to remember: always enjoy your beekeeping, never let the hive numbers rise until the job becomes drudgery, or keep bees whose temper reduces your satisfaction at opening a hive and looking at them.

Dealing with Pests

Every gardener will find pests and diseases affecting plants in the garden, and a range of pesticides is available to control them. The word pesticide is used not only to cover insecticides but also other classes of chemicals which do not normally present a threat to the honey bee, including herbicides, fungicides and molluscicides. Some acaricides are used in the hive to control parasitic mites and are harmless to the honey bee if used correctly.

Chemicals developed specifically for the control of insects are most likely to cause problems for bees. Fungicides and herbicides are not formulated in the same way, and this, coupled with the fact that there is normally no need to use them on crops or weeds when they are in flower (which is of course the time when bees are most at risk) means they are usually less dangerous. However, there is a risk in using herbicides on low-growing plants, even when not in flower, because honey bees often collect water from herbage near, or a short distance from, the hives. There have been cases of bees being poisoned by collecting freshly applied herbicide. If it is necessary to use herbicides, they should be applied after the bees have finished flying for the day, preferably at a time when a heavy dew is unlikely to occur, so that the chemical will have been absorbed before morning.

Fungicides are usually safe as they can also be applied when the bees are not flying. Triforine is a safe material which can be used to control blackspot on roses and scab on apples.

Until relatively recently a wide range of chemicals was available for pest and disease control, but many have been removed from the market due to major concerns over the build-up of resistant pests, and danger to the environment and humans caused by chemicals. There has also been misuse on an amateur scale. The professional pest control industry still has access to a wider range of chemicals but amateur use of these is illegal. All chemicals should be used carefully, following the instructions and the suggestions given on the label. It is better to look instead at growing resistant varieties and providing the correct cultural conditions to control diseases.

CULTURAL CONTROL

This entails growing plants that are more able to resist pathogen attacks. Healthy plants are selected, grown in fertile soils in the correct situation with correct nutrient levels, irrigation and ventilation, and regularly checked for

AIM FOR A DISEASE-FREE GARDEN

1. **Good hygiene** removal of dead and rotting plant material, and clearance of places where dormant diseases and pests can hide.

2. **Rotating vegetable crops** prevents the build-up of pest and disease populations in the soil, and thorough cultivations which expose pests to natural predators such as birds.

3. **Resistant or tolerant** varieties of crops and flowers.

4. **Thorough and regular hand picking** of pests such as caterpillars. This can be very effective, and the use of a torch at night will expose many slugs and snails which you can then remove by hand.

5. **Attention to pest biology** helps by highlighting their weaknesses; for example, the carrot fly cannot fly above 1m (3ft) so a mesh barrier will keep it off your crop. Placing sticky grease bands around fruit trees stops winter moths creeping up them.

6. **Erecting fences** and barriers to keep out larger pests.

7. **Using repellents** and scaring devices which can put off cats and moles.

8. **Trapping** to reduce populations of mammals and smaller pests such as earwigs, codling moth caterpillars, weevils and slugs.

9. **Companion planting** which can be effective in pest control, e.g. planting nasturtiums with tomatoes to control whitefly, and marigolds to control eelworms.

early control of pest or disease. In addition, the following all contribute to a disease-free garden:

BIOLOGICAL CONTROL

This involves the active management of natural enemies (predators, parasites or pathogens) to increase their impact on pest populations. Habitats to encourage and increase hoverflies and ladybirds will help control aphids, and habitats for hedgehogs and frogs will decrease slug numbers. Identification and protection of beneficial animals is important for this to work. Many biological agents are produced and introduced to glasshouses, such as the parasitic wasp *Encarsia formosa* which controls glasshouse whitefly. Although many are not yet suitable for outdoor use, the pathogen Bacillus *thuringiensis* can be used by gardeners for cabbage white caterpillars as well as the control of waxmoth in stored comb from honey bee colonies. Pathogenic nematodes have been developed for use by the gardener, Phasmarhabditis *hermaphrodita* controls slugs and Heterorhabditis *megidis* is used for vine weevil control.

INSECTICIDES

Over the last twenty years all of the persistent organochlorine and many of the organophosphorus chemicals have been withdrawn and replaced by organic and synthetic pyrethroid insecticides.

Pyrethrum is a natural organic insecticide made from Chrysanthemum *cinerariaefolium*, controlling aphids, whiteflies, leafhoppers, thrips, beetles and small caterpillars. It is very safe to use and breaks down quickly. Because it does not persist on the plant very long, thorough wetting of the crop is important. **Pyrethrum is toxic to fish and bees** and so should only be used when the bees are not active. There is also a range of synthetic pyrethroids with similar characteristics to pyrethrum.

Rotenone (Derris) is an organic insecticide derived from Derris roots with similar characteristics to Pyrethrum, and it is used to control aphids, thrips, small caterpillars, sawflies, red spider mite, raspberry and flea beetles. **It is toxic to fish and bees**.

Imidacloprid is a chloronicotinyl insecticide which is taken into the plant and passes around its system (systemic) so that the pest takes it in with its food. It is used widely on container plants and is safer for bees as it is applied to the compost. It is effective against aphids, vine weevil, sciarid flies and possibly whitefly.

MOLLUSCICIDES

Metaldehyde and aluminium sulphate are used in slug control baits but are applied to the ground in the evening and so should not effect bees.

Further details may be obtained from a good reference books, and many garden centres will also give advice and supply leaflets as well as biological controls.

The experienced beekeeper will recognise cases of poisoning when large numbers of bees die at the hive entrance. It is not always caused by something the amateur gardener has done: it is a characteristic of the effect of spraying large areas of crop, particularly from the air. As farmers and growers are becoming more aware of the importance of wildlife conservation, and if there is the need to spray to do so with care and forethought, the position with regard to pesticide poisoning of bees is improving all the time.

GUIDELINES FOR SAFE USE OF PESTICIDES

1. **Always read the label carefully,** and follow the directions.

2. **Doubling the dose** will not double the effectiveness but may damage the plants.

3. **Only apply chemicals as a last resort.** The first sight of pest can usually be dealt with by squashing or hand removal, so keep a close watch on your plants.

4. **Do not apply pesticides** to plants in bloom which may be visited by bees or any other pollinating insects. Remember bees may also be visiting nearby flowering weeds. If you must spray flowering plants do so after the bees have stopped flying – the wind will have dropped and there is less spray drift. Using the lowest pressure will produce bigger droplets which are less prone to drift.

5. **If using on a small scale** it may be better to buy a ready-mixed spray, with an integral sprayer. They are a bit more expensive, but you will use only what you need, you can keep any surplus for later, and there is no disposal problem or danger of mixing the wrong proportions.

6. **Store all chemicals safely,** away from sunlight and frost and in a locked shed, away from children and pets. Do not transfer or store chemicals in soft drink or unlabelled containers as children have been known to drink from them.

7. **If mixing your own spray,** use separate sprayers for herbicides and pesticides to prevent traces of herbicide damaging plants. Clean out sprayers thoroughly, immediately after use. Wash out empty containers and dispose of them as advised by your local authorities. Do not contaminate the environment, especially waterways, by pouring away surplus chemicals into nearby streams or rivers. Always try to estimate as accurately as possible the amount needed, as then there is no surplus and no problem of safe disposal.

8. **Do not use chemicals** which are produced for the commercial grower. This can be dangerous as well as illegal: commercial growers have to gain a spraying certificate before using such materials.

9. **Do not use aerosols** intended for greenhouse use outside, as the tiny droplets will remain in suspension in the air for a considerable time and drift widely on even the calmest day.